THE NEW ENCYCLOPEDIA OF
WATERCOLOUR
TECHNIQUES

THE NEW ENCYCLOPEDIA OF
WATERCOLOUR
TECHNIQUES

DIANA CRAIG & HAZEL HARRISON

Search Press

A QUARTO BOOK

Published in 2011 by Search Press Ltd
Wellwood
North Farm Road
Tunbridge Wells
Kent TN2 3DR

Previously published as *The Encyclopedia of
Watercolour Techniques* by Search Press, 2004

Copyright © 2004, 2011 Quarto Publishing plc

ISBN   978 1 84448 649 6

QUAR.EWT2

Conceived, designed and produced by
Quarto Publishing plc
The Old Brewery
6 Blundell Street
London N7 9BH

Senior Editor: Lindsay Kaubi
Art Editor: Jacqueline Palmer
Designer: Julie Francis
Art Director: Caroline Guest
Photographers: Paul Forrester,
Colin Bowling, Jon Wyland, Phil Wilkins
Picture Researcher: Sarah Bell
Creative Director: Moira Clinch
Publisher: Paul Carslake

Colour separation by Modern Age Repro House
Ltd, Hong Kong
Printed in China by 1010 Printing International

10 9 8 7 6 5 4 3 2 1

CONTENTS

ABOUT THE NEW EDITION

Artists have been painting in watercolour for centuries, yet this traditional and time-honoured medium can also be one of the most exciting and innovative. This third edition of *The New Encyclopedia of Watercolour Techniques* covers the same methods as in the previous editions but offers a wealth of new material too.

The book opens with a gallery of watercolour paintings by a number of different artists, demonstrating the huge array of styles and effects that can be achieved. This is then followed by a new section offering practical information on tools and materials, and advice on setting up a working space and on working methods.

The third chapter is the key section of the book: the techniques. All the traditional methods are shown here, from laying washes and working wet-in-wet to reserving highlights and lifting out, along with more unusual techniques such as spattering, feathering and creating texture with clingfilm and aluminium foil, for those who wish to experiment with the medium. Clear step-by-step pictures and text explain each process, and these are often accompanied by an additional gallery piece showing the technique in use.

The techniques chapter also includes useful features not available in the previous edition. Tips flag up points to watch for and suggest how to get the best results from each method; suggested applications offer ideas on where a technique might be most successfully applied; and cross-references link similar processes, to encourage greater creativity and exploration.

This edition includes a new fourth chapter, outlining a number of key principles and practices that every artist needs to know, from understanding colour and tone, working with light and shade, and creating spatial depth, through to developing a personal style, knowing the rules of good composition, and dealing with practicalities such as planning the order of your work.

This new encyclopedia includes everything a painter needs to know, and offers those other essential factors too – ideas and inspiration – to encourage you to pick up your brush and explore the delights of painting in watercolour.

GALLERY

The aim of the gallery is to whet your appetite by demonstrating just how versatile watercolour is as a medium. It is suited to every subject, and adaptable to every style. The examples here include minutely detailed architectural subjects, photo-realistic still lifes and flat, graphic depictions of flowers, as well as exuberant uses of washes, glazes and line.

LETTING THE PAINTING DEVELOP
Seduction by Ann Smith
The twin challenges of this painting were first having to work on a very large scale, and second starting without any precise subject matter in mind. Ann Smith has more or less allowed the painting to have its own way, working initially wet-in-wet with a 10cm (4in) brush, then drying the paper and adding more layers until she saw the image beginning to emerge.

PAINTING FLESH

Back by Keith M. Kennedy

For this painting (above), Keith M. Kennedy has given a lovely softness to the flesh by working with a carefully controlled wet-in-wet technique, using line in places to define the forms and details. Notice how he has brought in touches of vivid red on the hip and buttocks to tie the figure in with the drape below the body.

USING GLAZES

Exotic Friends by Ann Smith

This exquisite painting (right) demonstrates one of the key characteristics of watercolour – its transparent luminosity. Ann Smith has exploited this by building her painting up with a series of thin glazes that allow the whiteness of the paper to glow through – the painting looks as if it is almost lit from behind. The dark background throws the glazes into even lighter relief.

ADDING INTEREST

Tigger and Griffin by Keith M. Kennedy
Often a figure will give a touch of extra interest to a landscape. Here, the artist has used his cat in much the same way, so that the moving animal clearly in search of prey contrasts with the forever-immobile stone griffin. The cat provides a strong focal point, drawing the eye into the picture.

FAMILIAR SUBJECTS
The Old Harbour, Jakobstad
by Terry Jarvis
The artist returns to this subject over and over (right), always finding inspiration. As with his other paintings, this picture was completed on the spot, the endless hours of Finnish daylight giving him a major advantage. He has used a range of techniques – wet-in-wet, graded wash and wet-on-dry – and the use of tonal interchange gives the painting great impact.

EXPLOITING TECHNIQUES
Ionian Paradise by D.R. Gawthorpe
For this carefully planned and highly ambitious painting (left), the artist has used almost every watercolour technique including spattering, dry-brush and various masking methods. The water was built up in layers, and for the final overpainting, white acrylic was mixed with the watercolour.

RENDERING TEXTURES

Sleepers by David Poxon

David Poxon is fascinated by texture, and has chosen his subject (below) with this as his primary concern. He works on heavy paper, using the full range of watercolour techniques including lifting out, reserving whites, spattering and scumbling. Small highlights are achieved by scratching out.

CREATING HIGHLIGHTS

Contained by Denny Bond

In this almost photorealistic piece (facing page), the artist began by masking the condensation drops on the interior of the terrarium, and determining which other highlights should remain white. Colours and tones were then worked up, using washes and painting both wet-in-wet and wet-on-dry. Finally, the masking was removed and additional highlights scratched out with a knife.

PAINTING ARTIFICIAL LIGHT

Golden Celebration by Sally Robertson
Named after the rose itself, this watercolour (below) is as much about the light as the subject itself. Sally Robertson has used Cadmium Yellow painted wet-in-wet and diffused with magentas for the transitions from light to dark. The highlight on the lamp is the reserved white of the paper, and the roses have been painted petal by petal wet-on-dry.

CHOOSING AN UNUSUAL SETTING

Sweet Peas in a Tumbler
by Ronald Jesty
We are so conditioned by the idea of 'correct' settings for flower pieces and still lifes that the idea of placing a vase of flowers on a newspaper (above) seems almost heretical. But it works perfectly, with the newspaper images providing just the right combination of geometric shapes and dark tones to balance the forms and colours of the sweet peas.

USING INTENSE COLOUR
Rhododendrons and Pearls by Marjorie Collins
There is nothing wishy-washy about this dynamic image (left). Marjorie Collins has built up the intense colours by layering, working wet-on-dry. The brightest highlights were reserved as white paper, while the pale pinks on the right-hand blooms were reserved as an initial pale wash, allowed to dry, then painted around with darker tones.

WORKING IN LINE AND WASH
Wild Flowers by Brian Innes
This lively painting (right) reflects the artist's spontaneous response to the subject. Colour washes were first laid down to indicate the broad shapes. To give definition to the forms and to describe the detail, the artist then overlaid the washes with an ink drawing. The ink lines do not always follow the shape of the underlying patches of colour exactly, but this simply adds to the charm of the picture and reinforces the sense of free brushwork and spontaneity.

PAINTING INTRICATE DETAIL
Samarkand Mosque Doorway
by Moira Clinch
The artist was attracted to the contrasting textures and patterns in and around this doorway. The intricate tilework, the rough, chalky textures of the restored plaster and the weatherbeaten wood of the door appealed to the artist but required a mixture of painting techniques. Working from a detailed pencil sketch of the tiles, done *in situ*, and later from a photograph in the studio, she used various blues and earth colours to build up the image, using transparent glazes and working wet-on-dry. Sunlit areas of the tiles were painted directly onto the white paper.

WORKING FROM REFERENCES
Red Cross Hospital, Aix-en-Provence
by Catherine Brennand
This artist specialized in architectural subjects, and because she worked on a large scale, she used photographs and drawings rather than painting on the spot. In this painting (left), she has used wet-in-wet and spattering to build up the textures and give a lively freshness to the picture.

CREATING TEXTURE
Grand Canal by Catherine Brennand
Here (right) the same artist as above demonstrates a sensitive response to the contrast between the almost tactile texture of the crumbling Venetian walls and the crisply delineated plasterwork around the windows and balustrades.

TOOLS AND MATERIALS

Paints, paper and brushes are the watercolourist's essential toolkit. A sound knowledge of the materials that are available, their uses and the effects they can produce will make painting a more enjoyable process and ensure better results. There are other practical concerns to consider too, such as caring for tools, setting up a workspace, what equipment to buy – and learning those tips and tricks that can save time and make for greater artistic success. The following pages give information and advice on all the tools and materials the watercolour painter will need.

CHOOSING PAINTS

WATERCOLOUR HAS MANY ADVANTAGES OVER OTHER MEDIA AND PERHAPS THE GREATEST IS THAT YOU NEED ONLY A SMALL AMOUNT OF RELATIVELY INEXPENSIVE EQUIPMENT TO GET STARTED. IN FACT, THE ESSENTIAL MATERIALS FOR PAINTING IN WATERCOLOUR ARE JUST PAINT, PAPER, BRUSHES AND CLEAN, CLEAR WATER.

Types of watercolour

Before you buy your paints, you'll need to decide first between tubes and pans. Both have their merits. Pans are easier to carry around because you simply slot them into your paintbox. Tubes have to be carried separately, and the colours squeezed out as needed. Tubes are better when you need to mix up a lot of paint for washes.

TUBE PAINTBOX

If you have decided on tube paints, there are advantages to keeping them in a box. First, it's a neat way of storing and protecting them; and second, the troughs in the lid can act as a mixing palette. However, you should avoid boxes pre-fitted with a selection of colours. You won't know whether they are good quality, and you may well find yourself stuck with colours you don't need. It's better to buy an empty box that can be filled with colours that you have personally chosen.

PANS

All watercolours contain gum arabic to keep them moist, so don't be put off pans because you think they may dry up. Pans are available in whole and half-sizes. Try a half-pan if you are unsure about a colour. There is a wide range of paintboxes designed to hold pans and half-pans, which can be removed and replaced when used up. Like the tube paintbox, the lid can be used as a palette.

TUBES

Regular tubes of watercolour are quite small. Some manufacturers make larger sizes, but these are not necessary – it takes a long time to get through even a regular tube. Good-quality paints can be kept indefinitely as long as you remember to screw the caps back after use.

Selection of starter colours: Cadmium Red Deep, Alizarin Crimson, Ultramarine, Viridian, Yellow Ochre, Raw Umber, Payne's Gray, Lemon Yellow Deep, Cadmium Lemon, Cerulean Blue.

Coloured inks

ACRYLIC PAINTS AND INKS

As you build up your collection of materials, it's useful to add acrylics and inks to widen the range of results you can achieve. Both media can be used in combination with traditional watercolour, with interesting results. Thinned with water, acrylic paint behaves much like watercolour. Choose water-soluble or waterproof ink depending on the effect you want.

Tubes of acrylic, in standard and metallic colours

CHOOSE THE BEST QUALITY

Whether you opt for tubes or pans, be sure to buy artist's-quality watercolours. These are worth the extra cost because they are pigment-rich, providing greater vibrancy and depth of colour. Don't be tempted by the inexpensiveness of special 'sketching sets' or 'students'' colours; they may be inferior paints that will not produce the vibrancy you are after. Regard your initial outlay as a one-off investment; a tube or pan of paint will last a long time and, although you may sometimes need to replace an individual colour, you'll never have to buy a whole set again.

Tubes of gouache

GOUACHE PAINTS

Gouache paints are an opaque version of watercolours, which can be used more thickly and sometimes in combination with the transparent colours. Gouache white, in particular, is a useful alternative to Chinese white for adding highlights or thickening paint for certain effects. Gouache is sold in tubes, jars or bottles.

Zinc White gouache

Bottles of gouache

Titanium White watercolour

Chinese White watercolour

Jar of gouache

IRIDESCENT AND PEARLESCENT PAINTS

Glowing, luminescent watercolour paint has been in use for centuries, but now a whole new range of paints is available to enrich the artist's palette further and produce some exciting and unusual effects

At one time, the artist had few choices with regard to metallic and luminescent effects beyond conventional pigment colour. Then, in the 1960s, the automotive industry began developing various mineral-based, interference and iridescent pigments of great durability.

Now, artists' paint manufacturers use this technology to create new colours – every year new ones are released and others discontinued. These two pages provide a survey of some of the exciting and relatively recent developments within the industry, but you should also regularly check the catalogues and websites of all the manufacturers for their latest launches.

USING IRIDESCENT PAINT

Fish Pond by Shari Hills
In this exquisite painting (left), Shari Hills has used delicate watercolour glazes to depict a watery world. She has then dabbed on spots of iridescent colour for the sparkles on the water surface and the sheen where the fish scales catch the light. As with any special medium or technique, a 'less is more' treatment works best. Just a few iridescent accents are much more effective than an overall application.

IRIDESCENT PAINTS

Paints that contain coated mineral particles as well as a tinting pigment are called 'iridescent'. The optical phenomenon of a change in hue occurs according to the angle of observation. The example here shows iridescent paints applied over both a dark band of Ultramarine Turquoise and Napthamide Maroon (above) and white paper (below). Notice how some iridescents fail to cover the dark, whereas others create a gauze-like sheen and nearly disappear over white paper.

INTERFERENCE AND PEARLESCENT PAINTS

Transparent paints that contain uncoated mica particles and are not mixed with another pigment are nearly invisible on white paper. The optical phenomenon of colour is visible only when painted over a dark undercolour. Here, nine interference and pearlescent paints have been applied over both dark undercolour and white paper. Notice that all are very nearly invisible over the white paper and only appear when painted over the dark.

Blue Silver | Scarab Red | Sunstone | Moonstone | Russet | Topaz

Red | Lilac | Copper | Blue | Green | Silver | Gold | Pearlescent Shimmer | Pearlescent White

MEDIA

A wide range of effects and techniques can be created by simply mixing clean water with good-quality watercolour paint. There are also several watercolour media available, which can be used to good effect.

GUM ARABIC is one of the major constituents of watercolour paint. It not only helps bind the pigment, but also contributes to the transparency and depth of the colour. Gum arabic can be added to paint in two ways: a few drops can be placed in the general mixing water, or it can be added to specific washes or mixes only. Adding gum arabic will make your colours more transparent, give them greater depth and imbue them with a slight gloss. More importantly, it will increase the solubility of the dry paint, making corrections possible.
Advantages: makes a number of textural effects possible, and makes corrections easier.
Disadvantages: over-use can result in paint drying with a gloss finish; heavy use can cause paint to crack when applied too thickly.
Cost: inexpensive, when used sparingly.

WATERCOLOUR MEDIUM behaves like – and has similar qualities to – gum arabic, but it also improves the flow of washes. It can be added to the mixing water, or used selectively on individual washes.
Advantages: increases the brilliance and transparency of colours.
Disadvantages: over-use can result in areas of work drying to an unsightly gloss finish.
Cost: relatively inexpensive.

IRIDESCENT MEDIUM adds a pearlescent effect to watercolour. Add when the wash or colour is being mixed, or apply over the paint once it is dry. It is shown off to best effect when mixed with transparent colours and applied over a dark background.
Advantages: particularly useful for design and decorative work.
Disadvantages: can contaminate paints, or show up in parts of the work in which it is not required.
Cost: relatively inexpensive.

TEXTURE MEDIUM contains small particles suspended in a gel. It can be mixed with wet paint and then applied, or it can be brushed directly onto paper and then worked over with colour. With patience, multiple layers can be built up to create pronounced textural effects.
Advantages: increases the capability of the watercolour medium.
Disadvantages: brushes can be ruined if not cleaned thoroughly.
Cost: relatively inexpensive.

GRANULATION MEDIUM causes watercolour to granulate – an effect that occurs naturally with certain relatively coarse blue and earth pigments that separate out from a wash and settle into the texture of the support, giving a granular, textured effect.
Advantages: gives added drama.

Disadvantages: can lose effectiveness if overdone.
Cost: relatively inexpensive.

PERMANENT MASKING MEDIUM can be used in two ways: it can be applied undiluted onto the support; once dry, the medium is invisible, but it will isolate the masked area and repel any washes painted over it. Alternatively, the medium can be mixed with paint. When dry, it will resist any further washes.
Advantages: does not have to be removed, and thus allows for the creation of complex layers of masking.
Disadvantages: impossible to remove or alter once an area as been treated and masked.
Cost: relatively inexpensive.

LIQUID FRISKET is also known as masking fluid, and is neither an additive nor a medium. It is a liquid latex solution that is painted onto the support. Once dry, it isolates the area from any unwanted washes painted over it. Once the wash is dry, the masking fluid is removed by gentle rubbing.
Advantages: can be applied in any number of ways, and the fluid colour makes it is easy to see masked areas.
Disadvantages: may tear the surface if care is not taken when removing the dry fluid from the support. Also, brushes can be ruined if not cleaned thoroughly.
Cost: relatively inexpensive.

Granulation medium   Watercolour medium

Texture medium   Permanent masking medium   Masking fluid

Iridescent medium   Gum arabic

Masquepen: masking fluid can be applied with a masquepen, a bottle with a built-in applicator that allows for precise mark-making.

BRUSHES AND OTHER TOOLS

BRUSHES COME IN A RANGE OF SHAPES, SIZES AND FIBRES – THE CHOICE DEPENDS ON PERSONAL TASTE AND THE EFFECT THAT THE ARTIST WANTS TO CREATE. BUT BRUSHES ARE NOT THE ONLY TOOLS FOR MARK-MAKING.

Sable brushes with various heads

TYPES OF BRUSHES

There are three main shapes of watercolour brush: rounds, flats and mops. All are made in a range of sizes, usually identified by number but sometimes by their actual size (for example, 15mm or ½in). In most lines, the biggest brush is No.12 or No.14, and the smallest No.1, No.0 or even No.00.

As well as size and shape, the fibre from which the brush head is made determines its properties, and you should take this into account when choosing which brushes to buy.

Sable brushes This is the traditional fibre of choice for watercolour brushes. Sable is springy and resilient, and forms firm tips that point well – a top-quality sable brush will return to a point with one flick of the wrist when wet. Sable also carries a large amount of colour, yet releases it quickly and cleans rapidly. On the down side, this fibre is expensive. However, if cared for properly, a sable brush should last for years.

Synthetic brushes A much cheaper option, synthetic-fibre brushes mimic many of the qualities of sable. They have their own distinct qualities and can point well, making them useful for detailed work. When changing from one colour to another, though, they are more difficult to clean. Successful, long-lasting synthetic brushes (made of nylon or a mixture of nylon and sable) are available, which have some of the qualities of sable but at a much lower cost.

Squirrel-hair brushes Also known as camel hair, these can hold even larger amounts of colour than sable and therefore are useful as wash brushes in the larger sizes. They lack both the firmness of sable and synthetic fibre and the controllability needed for accurate, detailed work. Their advantage is that they are a fraction of the cost of sable brushes. Composite sable/squirrel brushes are available too; less expensive than sable, they retain some of its qualities for controlled or detailed work.

Goat-hair brushes These large, flat brushes with very soft and long, whitish hairs are also known as hake brushes. They are useful for applying large amounts of colour rapidly, yet are gentle enough to cause minimum disturbance to any underlying colour. When wet, the long, straight edge of the tip can be used to paint a range of shapes.

Hogshair brushes Traditionally used in oil painting, these firm brushes are useful for lifting colour as well as applying large amounts where accuracy is not important.

Chinese brushes A useful and cheaper alternative to sable, these can create detail as well as superb flowing lines.

Synthetic brushes

Squirrel-hair brush

Hake goat-hair brush

Hogshair brushes

Chinese brushes

TIPS: CHOOSING BRUSHES

• When you are starting out, you don't need a vast range of brushes. One flat, square-ended brush and three rounds of different sizes, in a sable and nylon mix, will be enough to get you going. You can slowly build up your collection, according to personal taste and your pocket.

• Regardless of a brush's make-up, it should be resilient and springy. You can test this by wetting the brush to a point and dragging it lightly over your thumbnail; springy bristles will return to their original position.

• You also need your brushes to hold a good quantity of water. Test by loading the brush with water, then squeezing it out.

TIPS: CARING FOR BRUSHES

• Keep your watercolour brushes solely for watercolour painting.

• Do not leave the heads of your brushes standing in water – you will ruin them. Instead, stand them upright in a jar.

• Rinse your brush under running water after each painting session. Use a little soap if traces of dried colour stick to the end near the metal band. Reshape gently with your fingers.

• If you have to carry your brushes around, protect the points. Use an old ruler and a couple of rubber bands to make a splint for them, or use a purpose-made cylindrical container. Keep the brushes upright or the tips may bend.

OTHER MARK-MAKERS

Brushes are not the only mark-making tools available to the watercolourist. There are a range of others, from fairly conventional to experimental.

Sponge A small natural sponge, available from art shops, is an extremely useful piece of equipment. It can be used for applying colour, laying washes and making corrections as well as for cleaning up.

Cotton balls These serve much the same purpose as a sponge, although they do not have the same colour-retaining properties and tend to be drier in use.

Cotton buds These are good for lifting out small highlights, or for doing corrections.

Toothbrush An old toothbrush is the perfect tool for the spatter technique.

Clingfilm, bubble wrap, aluminium foil Usually found in the kitchen or stationery cupboard, all these materials can be pressed into wet paint to create surface texture.

PALETTES

If you store your watercolour pans or tubes in a paintbox, the lid will be designed for use as a mixing palette. An alternative is an individual palette, with recessed 'wells' to hold the colour and divisions to separate one colour from another. Palettes are available in china or more inexpensive plastic, which is light enough for outdoor work. However, if you don't want to go to the expense of buying a purpose-made palette, you could use an old plate (preferably white and unpatterned, so you can judge the mixes more accurately) – although because there are no troughs you won't be able to keep your colours separate so easily.

OTHER USEFUL TOOLS

• Paper towel – almost essential, for lifting out colour, wiping brushes and general cleaning up.

• Pencil and eraser, for preliminary drawing. A B-grade pencil is soft enough not to indent the paper.

• Pens – felt-tip and India ink nib – for line and wash.

• Gummed tape, for stretching paper (see page 27). Never be tempted to use masking tape for this.

• Craft knife or scalpel, and scissors.

• Wax candles or crayons, for the wax-resist technique.

• Water spray bottle, to soften colour or for spraying wet paint to create surface texture.

• Small, flexible palette knife, for mixing colour – a preferable alternative to mixing large quantities of a colour with a brush, which could shorten its life.

WATER JARS

You will also need a jar to hold water. Old, clean jam jars are fine for indoor work. If you are going to be working outdoors, use a lighter plastic pot with a lid.

PAPER

WATERCOLOURS ARE ALMOST ALWAYS PAINTED ON WHITE PAPER, WHICH REFLECTS BACK THROUGH THE THIN LAYERS OF PAINT, GIVING IT ITS LUMINOUS QUALITY. IT HELPS TO KNOW THE QUALITIES OF THE DIFFERENT WATERCOLOUR PAPERS IN ORDER TO ACHIEVE THE EFFECTS YOU WANT.

TYPES OF PAPER

The finest-quality watercolour paper is made by hand from pure linen rag. These papers are expensive, and if you are a beginner you won't need them. The papers you'll find in your local art supply store are machine-made. There are many different brands, all with slight variations, but they can all be divided into three groups.

Hot-pressed paper This is made smooth by passing it through heated rollers after it is made. Its smooth surface makes it ideal for detailed work, such as botanical painting, but it has none of the pleasing surface texture of rougher papers.

Cold-pressed paper To achieve its characteristic 'tooth', or surface texture, this paper is pressed between unheated rollers lined with felt mats. It is the most popular paper and is referred to as 'not surfaced', which means it hasn't been hot-pressed. It has a moderately rough texture, just enough for colour to drag off the brush and create many useful effects.

Rough paper Not pressed at all, this has a distinctly characteristic rough surface. This rough surface acts as a moderating influence and helps control the flow of pigment, contributing to an even finish, if desired. Alternatively, if pigment is used fairly dry, it can be dragged across the surface to produce many textures. Never underestimate the capacity of even the roughest paper to produce accurate, detailed work, especially on larger paintings to be viewed at a distance.

WEIGHTS OF PAPER

Sheets of watercolour paper come in different thicknesses. These are measured in weight – this is important because it dictates whether you will have to stretch them. The weight of paper is usually expressed in grammes per square metre. A thin, lightweight paper may be no more than 160gsm, while medium-weights start at 250gsm, with heavier weights at around 400gsm – although really heavyweights can go up to 600gsm or more. As a general rule, any paper heavier than around 400gsm can be used without stretching. The paper used in most watercolour pads is 250gsm, which you can just get away with using without stretching.

1 and 2: Handmade paper, 3: Hot-pressed paper, 4: Rough paper, 5: Cold-pressed paper, 6: Watercolour board.

FINDING THE RIGHT SIDE

Not all papers have watermarks but, if they do, this indicates that there is a 'right' and 'wrong' side. Hold the paper up to the light, and if you can read the watermark, this is the side to paint on.

STRETCHING PAPER

When paper becomes very wet, it has a tendency to buckle, and an uneven flow of paint will result. Often this does not matter, and the very unevenness can add vitality to a painting. At other times, more control is required; if that is the case, it is advisable to stretch the paper first, to ensure a flat, taut surface on which to paint. To stretch paper, you will need a drawing board, gummed tape, a sponge and a craft knife and scissors.

1 With dry hands, cut four strips of gummed paper tape, slightly longer than the sides of the painting paper. Then put the roll of gummed paper away in a dry place – it should always be handled with dry hands. Rule light pencil lines about 1cm (½in) from the edges of the paper to help you put the tape on straight.

2 Immerse the paper briefly in water in a bath, sink or plastic tray, turning it over once to make sure both sides are evenly wetted. Place the paper on a board and smooth it with a damp sponge to remove any creases or air bubbles.

3 Run the sponge over the paper strips to just dampen them. Using the sponge, neatly smooth the strips along the edges of the paper, following your pencil lines: The tape should overlap the edge of the paper by at least 6 mm (¼in). Trim the corners. Stand the board upright until the paper is completely dry. You can now paint on the paper. To remove the painting from the board, cut through the tape with a craft knife

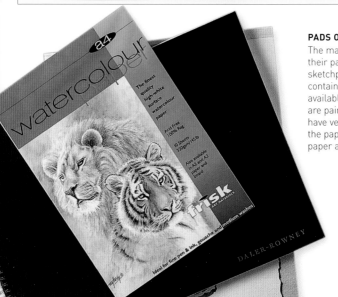

PADS OR SHEETS?

The major manufacturers produce their paper in large sheet and sketchpad form. The pads usually contain 10 or 12 sheets, and are available in a variety of sizes. If you are painting a large work, or if you have very specific requirements of the paper, it is better to buy your paper as a loose sheet.

USING WATERCOLOUR BOARD

If you have no time to stretch paper, you could use watercolour board, which is simply paper stuck to a firm backing.

SETTING UP A WORKING AREA

PAINTING WITH WATERCOLOUR CAN BE A REAL JOY, BUT TO MAKE THE EXPERIENCE AS PLEASURABLE AND SUCCESSFUL AS POSSIBLE, YOU NEED TO HAVE A WELL-ORGANIZED WORKING AREA.

Having a designated area in which to work is an ideal to aim for. Not only will it provide practical storage for your tools and materials, but it will also give your mind the subliminal message that you are taking your art seriously. Artists who work in acrylics or oils have the potential to work big but this isn't usually true of watercolourists, who don't therefore need vast studios. If you don't have a spare room, an unused corner or perhaps a well-lit landing are the kinds of spaces that can be put to good use.

Set up your workspace so that you can, as far as possible, look down on the paper you are painting on rather than viewing it at an angle. Distortion in a painting is often caused by the angle at which you are working. It's also important to step back often to assess your work (luckily watercolourists don't need as much space for this as oil painters who often have to stand quite a way back to view their enormous canvases). There is nothing more soul-destroying than finding that the painting you thought looked great close up does not work when seen at a distance.

LAMPS

Working lights need not form part of your 'starter kit', but you will need to consider suitable lighting if you intend to work in the evenings. Anglepoise lamps are useful because they can be angled to throw light exactly where you want it. They are available from good suppliers of graphic materials.

LIGHT BULBS

There is no substitute for daylight but it may not always be possible to paint during the day. If you have no choice but to paint by artificial light, avoid working under tungsten lighting; it has a yellow cast and distorts colour, flattens tone and reduces definition, and will make it harder for you to judge what you are doing. When you look at your painting the following morning, it may look quite different from the way it did the night before – and you may wonder why you did not notice that bright colour or that rather crude brushwork. Clear, bright, white lighting is a much more effective choice. Fluorescent and halogen are better than tungsten, but the best option of all are the blue, daylight-simulation bulbs that are the closest artificial approximation to daylight. They are available from art shops.

TIPS: STORAGE SOLUTIONS

• If you don't have a room or corner set aside just for painting, storing tools and materials can be a problem. One solution is to use one of those storage units on wheels, with drawers in which you can stash items away. The unit can be tucked into a corner or under a table when not in use and – if the top is big enough and the right height – it can double as a work surface when in use.

• To remain in pristine condition, sheets of paper, pads and card ideally need to be stored flat. Those lucky enough to have their own studios may have space for a plan chest in which to keep such items. If you do not have this luxury, you can use large portfolios for storage. Propped up vertically on their spines, portfolios take up little space and can be tucked out of sight until needed. Available from art shops, they come in a range of types and sizes, from the inexpensive to the pricey. Choose according to your needs and pocket.

• Cardboard cylinders or plastic tubes are fine for storing thinner papers. However, heavier-weight watercolour papers might crease if rolled, and are best stored flat.

USING AN EASEL

Watercolour is not like oil paint which stays where you put it – when it is wet watercolour runs. For this reason, you cannot use an easel for watercolour painting in the same way as you would for oils. Unless you actually want the paint to run to create a special effect, the easel should be tilted back sufficiently so that the paint remains where you apply it, but not so flat that it is difficult for you to see your work. Several easel designs have a tilt facility that allows you to adjust your board to a horizontal or near-horizontal angle for working, then adjust it back up to vertical for viewing. If you want to splash out, there are even easels specifically designed just for watercolour work.

Paper towels
Always have these on hand to mop up extra paint or water in a hurry.

Salt
This is a great way to add texture (see pages 88–89).

Light source
Good lighting is essential for any form of painting. The direction of the light source is important too. If you are right-handed, the light should come from the left (and from the right if you are left-handed), or your working hand will throw a shadow on your work.

Organization
Keep loose paints in a large box – buy one larger then you need, as you will probably buy more paints as your skills improve.

A working surface

It may seem obvious but having an adequate work surface often gets overlooked when setting up a painting space. It must be big enough to take water jars, paints, palette, brushes and any other materials and aids that you need – watercolour is a fast-drying medium so you need everything to hand. Your work surface may have to accommodate your painting board too. If you are painting at an easel, the work surface should be sited close by and be the appropriate height, so that all your materials and tools are easily within reach. If you are lucky enough to have a studio or designated painting corner, you can have a large table solely for this purpose. If not, a kitchen or even dining table will do, covered with newspaper to protect it.

Palettes and water pots
Keep water pots next to palettes to prevent water dripping on painting.

Hair dryer
Useful for speeding the drying process.

Cotton buds
For lifting out paint.

Bar of soap
For quick cleaning of brushes after masking.

Paper
The paper has been stretched onto a moveable board.

EASEL
An easel is not essential, but it is useful if you like to paint while standing. It must be adjustable so that the paper can lie almost flat. A table easel can also be useful if space is not available.

DRAWING BOARD
A board is important for supporting your paper. It needs to be firm – the wood should not be less than 4-ply – and it should be unstained and unpolished. (If it is stained, the stain sometimes comes off on the back of the paper; if it is polished, the gummed paper will not stick when you are stretching your paper.)

WORKING OUTDOORS

WORKING OUTDOORS, *EN PLEIN AIR*, CAN BE A REAL PLEASURE. HOWEVER, WHETHER YOU'RE DOING QUICK SKETCHES OR A COMPLETE PAINTING, IT NEEDS MORE ORGANIZATION THAN INDOOR WORK, SO PLAN YOUR PAINTING TRIPS CAREFULLY.

If you like painting away from home, it might be worth keeping a special kit ready for just this purpose, with all the tools and equipment you will need. Then all you'll need to grab before you go are paints, paper and brushes. Bear in mind, too, that you are going to have to carry the lot, so avoid anything that weighs too much. And a final word of warning: Be prepared for a little audience – of children especially – to gather to watch you at work. Most will be too impressed by your artistic skills to spot the odd 'mistake', so don't let this put you off what you are doing.

CHOOSING A LOCATION

Since you won't want to traipse around with your painting equipment looking for a good place to paint from, it's best to plan this in advance. You could explore the area the day before and choose your spot so that you go straight to it. If you're intending to complete an entire picture rather than making sketches, you might also consider doing the drawing on one day and painting on another. One of the difficulties of location work is coping with changing light; you may think you have the whole day to paint in, but the scene will have changed completely between morning and evening, so you'll have to work fast – remember Monet's haystack series of paintings and how the colours and tones changed depending on the time of day? If you've already done the drawing the day before, you can start on the painting immediately without wasting valuable time.

SEATING
A garden chair will provide you with seating, but may be too high for you to reach your materials on the ground comfortably. A specially designed sketching stool is better.

EASEL CARRIER
This piece of equipment is far from essential, but can be helpful if you have to walk long distances.

EASEL
You don't necessarily need an easel because you can paint with your board or sketchpad held on your lap. If you want to invest in an easel, make sure it's light enough to carry easily and that it can be adjusted so that the board is held near-horizontally. There are two main types – wooden ones and metal ones. They both weigh about the same and the height and angle can be adjusted.

SHADE
Watercolours dry very fast under a hot sun, and bright light on your paper will dazzle you, making it hard to see the colours. It's generally best to find a shady spot to work in. However, if you do have to work in the sun, it's wise to wear some form of hat or cap.

PAPER

For small, quick sketches you don't need to stretch paper. Use a watercolour pad or paper attached to a light piece of plywood or hardboard.

EQUIPMENT

You will also need the following pieces of equipment:
- Water container – any plastic bottle will do.
- Water pot – the non-spill ones (red top) are ideal.
- Brush holder – this is not essential but will protect your brushes.
- Paper towels, for wiping brushes, mopping up excess paint and cleaning up.
- Large plastic bags, to protect your work if it rains.

CHECKLIST

When painting outdoors, you won't be able to pop to the cupboard or kitchen to collect something you've forgotten, so you need to be extra-organized. Before you set off, check that you have the following:

- Brushes (you won't need many) ✓
- Paintbox or tubes ✓
- Mixing pans ✓
- Sketching block or light drawing board and sheets of paper ✓
- Drawing pins, masking tape or bulldog clips for securing sheets of paper (if using) ✓
- Bottle for carrying water ✓
- Jar or plastic pot for paint water ✓
- Pencil and eraser for preliminary drawing ✓
- Knife or sharpener for sharpening pencils ✓
- Sponges and paper towels, for applying paint, lifting out, and mopping up ✓
- Plastic bag to protect your work from rain ✓
- Sketching stool, or folding chair ✓
- Easel and easel carrier (optional) ✓
- Viewfinder (optional) ✓

USING A VIEWFINDER

When you're faced with a large expanse of scenery it can be very difficult to decide which bit to concentrate on. This is where a viewfinder, made from two L-shaped pieces of card, or a viewing frame – a rectangular window cut in a piece of cardboard – comes in. Hold it up at arm's length to isolate parts of the view, moving it around until you see the makings of a composition. Most artists use a viewfinder; some even take a picture frame out with them to assess how their painting will look when completed and framed!

TECHNIQUES

Watercolour can be both a challenging medium and an exciting one that offers huge scope for experimentation and unusual effects. Many techniques have been around for centuries and still form the foundation of watercolour work. These need to be mastered first – without knowing how to lay a wash or work wet-in-wet, for example, little progress can be made. But once you are familiar with these fundamental processes, you can add new ones to your repertoire – exploring wax resist or spattering, for example, or breaking up wet colour by sprinkling it with salt – and revel in all the effects that this endlessly adaptable medium offers. This chapter explains the whole range of techniques that are possible with watercolour, from the familiar to the lesser-known.

PRIMING PAPER

UNDERSTANDING HOW YOUR PAPER REACTS TO AND ABSORBS WATER AND PIGMENT IS CRITICAL TO YOUR SUCCESS WITH THE TECHNIQUES SHOWN IN THIS BOOK.

Think of it like this: if you prime wood before painting it, the top coat will go on more smoothly and successfully. It's the same with watercolour. Watercolour can be quite an unforgiving and temperamental medium. Once it is dry, it does not really like to be disturbed, or it will start to move around in ways you might not want. You need to control the flow of the paint by priming the paper first. Priming will not only help you to lay flatter washes or softer graded ones, but will also enable you to judge the receptivity of the paper more accurately.

You can apply this technique either to the whole of your painting – say, if you are going to lay down an overall pale, warm yellow wash for background warmth – or just to a selected area such as a sky.

LAYING A WATER WASH
1 On heavy watercolour paper or stretched paper, a large brush is used to apply clean water, with quick, even strokes. Clean water is important in watercolour painting so that reserved highlights and colours remain clear and unpolluted.

2 The paper starts to absorb some of the water, and some sits on the surface. There should be an even, wet shine on top. If the water starts to puddle too much, you can absorb the excess by dabbing with a paper towel.

3 If too much water has been applied over a larger area, the excess wetness can be blotted away by carefully placing paper towel flat down onto the paper.

4 If it is a cold day or time is limited, a hairdryer can be used to remove some of the moisture.

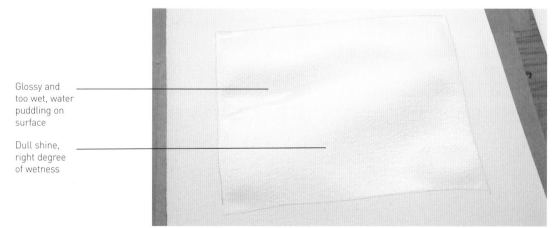

Glossy and too wet, water puddling on surface

Dull shine, right degree of wetness

JUDGING THE WETNESS
5 The aim is to let the paper dry to a semi-gloss, almost silk finish. This finish is important as the paint will go down more smoothly. The other reason is that a very wet surface will buckle too much, making it impossible to get a flat wash because the pigment will run into the troughs. Here, some areas are still a bit wet and glossy, but others are at the perfect stage to receive paint.

PRIMING AN AREA WET-ON-DRY

The technique can also be applied to areas of a picture that are already painted. A good sable brush pays off here, as it is so much gentler on the fragile pigment underneath.

1 The area that is to receive the secondary glaze is allowed to dry. Then, using a brush at an oblique angle so that it doesn't press too hard on the painted area, a layer of clear water is applied.

2 Care is taken to paint the water around and not across the details, or it will 'conduct' the paint into those parts.

3 Colour is dropped or softly washed on. The wet, receptive paper allows the colour to flood evenly over the area and around (but not across) the details.

6 An adequate amount of the desired colour is mixed up, then applied as a flat wash. The damp paper surface allows the paint to flow more easily, and makes it easier to move around, than if it was going directly onto dry 'virgin' paper. Not only does this produce flatter washes, but variegated washes will blend more smoothly too.

INTRICATE EDGES

The technique is especially useful for painting a clear sky above a complex, detailed horizon. If the paper is dry, it's very hard to paint around the complex horizon line and cover the sky with a flat or even a graded wash before the paint dries.

1 The artist draws in the horizon details, then turns the board upside-down – it is easier to work into the complex outline from below – and paints clear water around the details and all the way to the top of the painting. The paper is left to absorb the water and reach the 'silk' stage.

2 The artist lays a blue wash all over the sky, starting at the horizon. The paint flows over the damp area up to the dry edges, then stops. The artist takes care not to get grease from her hands on the paper as this will act as a barrier to water and paint.

FLAT WASH

THE WATERCOLOUR WASH IS ONE OF THE BASIC BUILDING BLOCKS OF WATERCOLOUR PAINTING, AND THE FLAT WASH IS THE SIMPLEST OF THESE. IT IS THE EASIEST METHOD FOR APPLYING COLOUR TO THE PAPER, AND PROBABLY THE VERY FIRST EXERCISE FOR THE BEGINNER IN WATERCOLOUR.

BLENDING DAMP WASHES
Company by Denny Bond
The darks of the cows are painted in. An almost but not quite flat wash has been used for the sky – it is slightly lighter and pinker just above the horizon. The background trees were painted while the wash was still damp so that they blend in with no hard edges.

The term 'wash' is a rather confusing one, because it implies a relatively broad area of paint applied flatly; however, it is also sometimes used by watercolour painters to describe each brushstroke of fluid paint, however small it may be. Here it refers only to paint laid over an area too large to be covered by one brushstroke.

Before applying a flat wash in watercolour, thinned gouache or acrylic, the paper is usually dampened to allow the paint to spread more easily. Tilt the board slightly, at an angle of no more than 30°, to allow the brushstrokes to flow into each other – but not so steeply that the paint dribbles down the paper.

Load the brush with paint, sweep it horizontally across the paper, starting at the top and immediately lay another line below it, working in the opposite direction. Keep the brush loaded for each stroke and continue working in alternate directions until the area is covered.

SUGGESTED APPLICATIONS
• Use for large, flat expanses of colour such as skies.
• Apply as a flat base colour to work into, wet-on-dry.

1 Starting with a wide brush, load enough diluted colour to make one stroke across the top of the paper. Tilting the board slightly towards you allows the paint to flow downwards.

TIPS: PAINTING THE INITIAL WASH

• Choose your brush carefully. A round brush forms a point when wet so should be at least a No.12; a flat brush, such as a hake, will make it easier to get an even result.

• Washes must be applied fast, so mix plenty of paint before you start – you always need more than you think.

• Do not overpaint an area while wet or it will result in an uneven wash.

2 Continue down the paper quickly, not allowing the paint to dry between strokes. Work back over uneven lines if necessary to even out any discrepancies in the wash.

3 Continue down to the base of the paper, tilting the board to encourage even flow of the pigment before it settles.

4 Here the paint has dried to a flat, even finish. Some pigments will granulate and produce a grainy effect. Get to know the paints in your palette before applying them to your painting.

WORKING AROUND INTRICATE SHAPES

Sometimes it is necessary to lay a wash around an intricate shape. You can mask off the shape or you can apply the wash around it. This is easier if you start at the bottom of the picture and work upwards, rather than from the top down, so turn your board upside-down before you start. If you are dampening the paper first, dampen it only up to the edge of the shape because the paint will flow into any area that is wet.

SEE ALSO

Stretching paper, page 27
Masking, pages 70–71
Toned ground, pages 90–91

USING A SPONGE

Some artists prefer to use a sponge for laying washes. For the most even results, the paper is first dampened with a clean sponge. The sponge is then dipped into the paint before each stroke and dragged evenly from one side of the paper to the other, until the whole surface is covered. Slight streaks where one band of colour meets the next will merge as the paint dries. If applied with a sponge, the paint tends not to run down the paper as it can with a brush.

1 A sponge is a useful piece of equipment in watercolour painting. Some artists prefer it to a brush for laying washes. Dampening the paper first gives the best results.

2 Place the board flat to dry. The bands of colour will flow together as the paint dries, and any streakiness will disappear.

GRADED WASH

A GRADED WASH IS SLIGHTLY MORE TRICKY TO ACHIEVE THAN A FLAT WASH, BUT IS AN IDEAL TECHNIQUE FOR CONVEYING THE SUBTLE CHANGES OF COLOUR AND TONE FOUND IN NATURE.

Colours in nature are seldom flat and uniform. A graded wash, that shifts in tone from dark to light, can give a more realistic effect than an area of flat tone or colour.

A graded wash is laid in the same way as a flat wash, the only difference being that more water is added to the pigment for each successive band of paint. It can be difficult to achieve a really even gradation because too much water in one band or not enough in another will result in a striped effect.

When applying a graded wash, keep the paint as fluid as possible so that each brushstroke flows into the one below, and never be tempted to work back into the wash if it does not come out as you wished. If this happens, don't be discouraged – one of the joys of the watercolour medium is its unpredictability; what may at first appear to be a mistake can become one of the defining qualities of the finished picture.

SUGGESTED APPLICATIONS

• Use for large, flat expanses of colour such as sky (dark higher up, paler at the horizon) or sea (darker at the horizon, paler towards the shore).

APPLYING THE WASH

1 A graded wash should be applied with a large brush, well loaded with plenty of water and paint. Starting at the top of the paper – where the colour will be most intense – a broad band of the paint mixture is applied to the surface. The brush is drawn straight across a couple of times to apply one band of colour below the other, as with the flat wash technique. Each new stroke will lift any excess water from the previous stroke.

LAYING A GRADED WASH
France Profond by Roger Pickett
Often, a graded wash is worked vertically, starting with the darkest tone at the top and fading towards the bottom. However, in this painting, the gradation is right to left. The artist first masked out the buildings and foreground, then ran a wash over the sky, with the most intense blue on the right progressively fading to the left. He did not worry too much about getting an even gradation but allowed the paint to dry slightly patchily to suggest subtle cloud shapes.

2 The brush is then dipped in clean water (rather than paint), and a band of diluted colour is applied below the still-wet previous band.

3 More water is added to the brush for each band of colour. Each band will be paler than the one before and will blend smoothly into it.

TIPS: COLOUR WASHES

• Because the paint has to become more and more diluted, you will need to have plenty of water on hand for this technique.

• Remember that each wash should be only one step lighter than the previous one, so don't dilute too quickly.

• Don't rinse the brush between bands of colour, as this prevents a smooth progression of colour flow.

4 The wash is left to dry without working back into it and spoiling the even gradation.

USING A SPONGE

It may be easier to apply a graded wash with a sponge. This gives greater control over the amount of water used in each successive band of colour, and thus can give better final results.

SEE ALSO

Stretching paper, page 27
Flat wash, pages 36–37

VARIEGATED WASH

A VARIEGATED WASH USES MORE THAN ONE COLOUR AND TAKES THE WASH TECHNIQUE ONE STEP FURTHER THAN EITHER FLAT OR GRADED WASHES.

The variegated wash technique is essentially the same as for the other types of wash, but – instead of the single colour of the flat wash or the variation in tone of a graded wash – it combines two or more colours. It is less predictable than either flat or graded, but you can achieve very exciting – if unexpected – results by allowing the colours to bleed into each other. Sunset skies are rendered especially well by a variegated wash, starting with blue at the top, blending down into yellow, with orange and red at the bottom. To achieve the effect, sufficient quantities of the colours are mixed on the palette, then applied in bands, one below the other, onto dampened paper. The dampness of the paper does the rest by causing the different colours to bleed into each other.

SUGGESTED APPLICATIONS
• Use for dramatic skies or, using different blues and greens, for expanses of sea.

MAKING LESS SAY MORE
Landscape by Adrienne Pavelka
In her lovely evocation of clouds and hills, Pavelka has deliberately suppressed any detail, letting the large, bold shapes speak for themselves to create a sense of grandeur and drama. She prefers to work on site whenever possible.

SEE ALSO
Stretching paper, page 27
Flat wash, pages 36–37
Graded wash, pages 38–39

APPLYING THE WASH

1 A large brush is used to apply several bands of a rich Ultramarine to the paper. The colour is brushed on wet-in-wet to achieve even coverage.

2 Working quickly wet-in-wet and using a cleaned brush, a band of red is brushed on, overlapping the still-wet blue so that the two colours bleed into each other. Further bands of red are applied, still working wet-in-wet.

3 The same process is used to lay the third colour of the variegated wash. The paint is then left to dry.

4 Three distinct bands of colour form this variegated wash, each blending softly into the adjacent colour. For a more subtle effect, the colours could be more closely related, for example, a yellow merging into an orange merging into a red.

MIXING PAINT

Have sufficient of each paint colour mixed and ready before you begin – the essence of a successful wash is to work quickly so you won't want to have to stop halfway to mix up more paint.

WET-ON-DRY

LAYING NEW, WET WASHES OVER
EARLIER, DRY ONES IS THE
CLASSIC WAY OF BUILDING UP
A WATERCOLOUR PAINTING.

Because it is difficult to achieve great depth of colour with a preliminary wash, the darker and richer areas of painting are achieved by overlaying colours in successive layers – a technique known as 'wet-on-dry'. The danger with wet-on-dry is that you can allow too many layers to accumulate and muddy the colours, so if you are working mainly in flat washes, always try to make the first one really positive. It is, of course, equally permissible to paint some parts of a picture wet-on-dry and others wet-in-wet – indeed some of the most exciting effects are achieved by combining the two methods.

In acrylic, wet-on-dry is the most natural way to work since acrylic paints dry very quickly, but gouache – although also fast-drying – presents more of a problem. To work wet-on-dry in gouache, begin by using the paint like watercolour (with water but no white) and gradually build up to thicker layers. One thick layer over another will result in a dull, muddy effect.

SUGGESTED APPLICATIONS
• Work wet-on-dry where you want to build up richer tones.
• Use where you want to bring greater definition and sharpness to parts of a painting.

DRYING

One of the more irritating aspects of watercolour work is that of having to wait, sometimes for long periods, for paint to dry before the next colour is added. When working wet-on-dry, it is perfectly permissible to use a hairdryer to hasten the process (see page 34). However, avoid using it on really wet paint because you may find you are blowing a carefully placed wash all over the paper.

LEADING THE EYE
Garden Things by Moira Clinch
In a sensitive response to the watercolour medium, Moira Clinch has cleverly combined wet-in-wet with wet-on-dry. To lead the eye to the top third of the painting, with the brilliant blue and red of the pot and geraniums, and the light, spiky foliage, she has created crisp edges, while the lower part of the picture has been painted selectively wet-in-wet.

PAINTING THE WASHES
1 A bright yellow wash is laid down over the outline of the bird. While still wet, the edges of the painted area are feathered with a damp brush, pulling the paint to create varying degrees of transparency. When completely dry, washes of translucent orange are laid over the yellow.

ADDING SHAPES

2 The spaces between the leaf veins are painted with a combination of green, translucent orange and Lemon Yellow. The hard edges that define the leaf shape are retained, but the edges along the veins are lightly feathered.

3 The blue sky background is created by applying irregularly shaped dabs of Cerulean Blue: some edges of the blue dabs are pulled with a clean damp brush, leaving a few hard edges and some unpainted areas. Note how the graded washes and areas of unpainted white paper create depth.

ADDING FINE DETAILS AND TEXTURES

4 To maintain crisp edges, black and other deep-value colours should be painted onto a dry surface to prevent them from bleeding into adjacent colours. Small areas of colour and fine details are worked with a short-bristled, flat brush. Here, black mixed from green and crimson was brushed on with short strokes to depict the fine texture of the bird's feathers.

5 Fine strands of grass, string and horsehair make up the nesting material. A long, flexible rigger brush is ideal for applying wet paint in fine lines and squiggles. Any masking fluid that was applied in the nest area before the painting was begun is removed at this stage.

6 A rigger and a No.2 round brush are used to further define the strands of nesting material. The versatility of wet-on-dry technique allows the artist to obtain saturated colours next to thin washes. Sharp edges bring the subjects forward while softened edges retreat into the background.

SEE ALSO

Wet-in-wet, pages 44–45
Brushwork, pages 64–65

WET-IN-WET

THIS IS A TECHNIQUE THAT IS ONLY
PARTIALLY CONTROLLABLE, BUT IT IS
A VERY ENJOYABLE AND CHALLENGING
ONE FOR PRECISELY THIS REASON,
ALLOWING THE WATERCOLOUR ARTIST
TO TAKE ADVANTAGE OF THE 'HAPPY
ACCIDENTS' THAT RESULT.

Working wet-in-wet means exactly what its name implies – applying each new colour without waiting for earlier ones to dry, so that they run together with no hard edges or sharp transitions. Any of the water-based media can be used, providing no opaque pigment is added, but in the case of acrylic, it is helpful to add retarding medium to the paint to prolong drying time.

The paper must first be well dampened and must not be allowed to dry completely at any time. This means, first, that you must stretch the paper (unless it is a really heavy one of at least 400gsm); and second, that you must work fast. An alternative method is to drop colour into a wash that is still very wet so that the wetness of the paint itself allows the new colour to spread.

Paradoxically, when you keep all the colours wet, they will not actually mix, although they will bleed into one another. Placing a loaded brush of wet paint on top of a wet wash of a different colour is a little like dropping a pebble into water; the weight of the water in the new brushstroke causes the first colour to pull away.

The danger with painting a whole picture wet-in-wet is that it may look altogether too formless and undefined. The technique is most effective when it is offset by edges and linear definition, so when you feel you have gone as far as you can, let the painting dry, then take a long, hard look at it and decide where you might need to sharpen it up.

SUGGESTED APPLICATIONS
• Use the soft, loose forms to suggest flowers, foliage and tree shapes.
• Wet-in-wet also works well for billowing cumulonimbus cloudscapes.

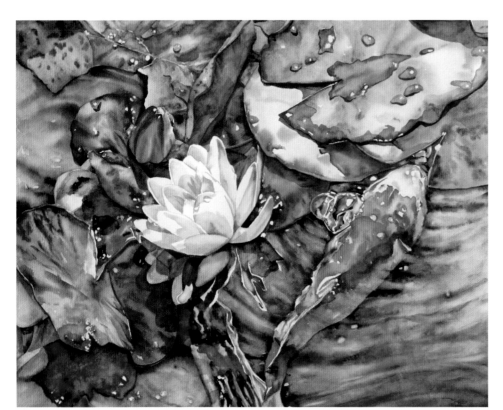

SELECTIVE WET-IN-WET
Julie by Sally Robertson
In all her paintings, Robertson works wet-in-wet within carefully defined areas, and this painting is no exception. In the water, a rainbow of freely applied colours capture the movement and suggestion of fish below the surface. The lily and the bubbles were painted wet-on-dry.

EXCESS PAINT

If the colour runs too much, or bleeds into an area where you don't want it, you can gently lift out the excess colour with a dry brush, cotton bud or tissue (see Lifting Out, pages 56–57).

2 A wash of yellow-green is flowed in over the background. The artist works quickly to achieve an even effect. This process needs care as the more paint there is on the brush, the more will transfer to a wet surface, leading to some large, unwanted patches of colour. When a narrower area is to be painted, dabbing the brush onto a paper towel first will remove some of the excess paint and make it possible to work more precisely.

APPLYING THE FIRST WASH

1 Having completed a detailed drawing showing the patterning of the plumage, and with the board tilted at approximately a 30° angle, the artist applies a wash to the head of the parrot, then adds shading and definition, working wet-in-wet so that the colours blend and blur. The brighter colour is applied with a repeating side-to-side, top-to-bottom brushstroke. The remaining plumage is painted in the same way.

4 The artist continues working over the painting to complete the details. Note how the wet-in-wet technique gives a beautifully soft effect on the breast feathers.

3 The shadows and outlines of the feathers need to be soft and blurry, not hard-edged. Even if the underlying wash has already dried, it is possible to re-wet the surface and work wet-in-wet, as here, to achieve the required effect.

SEE ALSO

Lifting out, pages 56–57

BLENDING

TO ACHIEVE A SOFT, GRADUAL TRANSITION FROM ONE COLOUR OR TONE TO ANOTHER, THE WATERCOLOUR ARTIST CAN CHOOSE FROM A NUMBER OF DIFFERENT TECHNIQUES.

SEE ALSO

Wet-in-wet, pages 44–45
Dry-brush, pages 68–69

BLENDING WITH SMALL STROKES

Plums in a Dish by Ronald Jesty
In this painting, the artist has dabbed on a number of different colours so that they blend subtly into each other, to convey the rich and complex colouring of the plums and their rounded shapes. In contrast, the shadows beneath have been allowed to form hard edges.

Blending colours or tones is a slightly trickier process with water-based paints than with oil paints or pastel, because watercolour paint dries more quickly. One option is to work wet-in-wet, keeping the whole area damp so that the colours flow into one another. This a lovely method for rendering amorphous shapes such as clouds, but is less suitable for precise effects, such as those you might need in portraits, because you cannot control the medium sufficiently – you might find that a shadow intended to define a nose spreads haphazardly out across the cheek.

To avoid the hard edges where a wash ends or meets another wash, brush or sponge the edge lightly with water before it is dry. To convey the roundness of a piece of fruit, for example, use the paint fairly dry, applying it in small strokes rather than broad washes. If unwanted hard edges do form, they can be softened by 'painting' along them with a small sponge or cotton bud dipped in a little water.

The best method for blending acrylics is to keep them fluid by adding retarding medium.

This allows for very subtle effects, as the paint can be moved around on the paper.

Opaque gouache colours can be laid over one another to create soft effects, though too much overlaying of wet colour may muddy the earlier layers. One way to avoid this is to use the dry-brush technique, applying the paint thickly with the minimum of water.

SUGGESTED APPLICATIONS

• Use to create soft effects in amorphous shapes such as clouds.
• Use to create a sense of three-dimensional form and definition, for example, in portraits or still lifes.

WETTING THE PAPER
1 First, an entire petal area is wetted with clear water.

2 While the paper is wet, yellow is painted on the interior of the petal and allowed to bleed out towards the edges. Gold is then added to indicate the shadowed centre of the petal.

TILTING THE PAPER

3 The paper is tilted downwards so that the colours can further blend into each other, while flowing to the outside.

4 While still wet, deep pink is added to the outside edges of the petals. The paper is turned around to let the pink bleed into the petal interior, pulling the colour into the clear water that was initially laid onto the paper.

ADDING THE FINISHING TOUCHES

5 Once the paint is dry, the edges of the petal are re-wet and then once again saturated with deep pink. As the new layer of paint dries, petal lines are very lightly painted in using a fine brush.

6 The petal is nearly finished. Final touches include lifting out colour with a cotton bud where highlights are needed.

7 The remaining petals are worked in the same way. The hard edges of the petals contrasting with the soft blending on their inner surfaces, along with the blurry background, really make the rose stand out.

Katrina Small

HARD EDGES

ONE OF THE DEFINITIVE QUALITIES OF
WATERCOLOUR IS ITS TENDENCY TO
FORM A HARD EDGE, RATHER LIKE A
TIDEMARK, WHEREVER IT MEETS A DRY
SURFACE. THIS QUALITY IS ONE OF THE
CHARMS OF THE MEDIUM.

A wet watercolour wash laid on dry paper forms a shallow pool of colour that, if left undisturbed, will form hard edges as it dries. This can be alarming to the novice, but it is one of the characteristics of the medium that can be used to great advantage. By laying smaller, looser washes over previous dry ones, you can build up a fascinating network of fluid, broken lines and shapes that not only help to define form but give a sparkling quality to the work. This is an excellent method for building up irregular, natural forms such as clouds, rocks or ripples on water.

You will not necessarily want to use the same technique in every part of the painting. A combination of hard and soft edges describes the subject more successfully and gives more variety. Soft edges can be created by working wet-in-wet; using a sponge, paintbrush or cotton bud dipped in clean water to remove excess paint; or by dragging or pulling a wash over dry paper with either a brush or sponge, which will prevent the paint from pooling and drying to a hard edge.

SUGGESTED APPLICATIONS
• Use for foliage, clouds, ripples on water or wherever a strongly textural effect is required.

SEE ALSO
Back runs and blossoms, pages 52–53

PAINTING THE FOLIAGE

1 The artist starts with a light pencil drawing to act as a guide for a painting of a forest. He then begins to drop in colour for the foliage, applying wet washes to dry paper and leaving the paint to dry naturally and form hard, ragged edges.

2 Drops of additional colour are applied on top, and again left to dry to create a patchy texture reminiscent of foliage.

EXPLOITING HARD EDGES

The natural tendency of watercolour to form hard edges can be exploited for graphic effect, as shown in these two still-life paintings of the same subject. The first painting uses a more traditional approach, with softly blended colours and tones. In the second painting, the artist has chosen to create an almost collage-like impression with her use of hard edges, strong shapes and dramatic tonal contrasts.

BACKGROUND AND FOREGROUND

3 When the foliage is dry, the artist carefully paints in the background, using the pencil outlines as a guide.

ADDING THE FINAL TOUCHES

5 When the other parts of the painting are dry, the artist fills in the trunks and branches with a solid, dark colour that contrasts well with the filtered-light effect of the foliage.

4 After painting in a base colour for the foreground and leaving this to dry, the same technique used for the foliage is applied. Spots of different browns are dropped in and left to form hard edges suggestive of the leafy woodland floor.

6 The finished picture demonstrates how effective this simple technique can be in conveying the texture of leaves. The solid trunks offer a contrast and accentuate the foliage effect.

GLAZING

BUILDING UP COLOUR AND TONE BY OVERLAYING TRANSPARENT WATERCOLOUR WASHES IS SOMETIMES REFERRED TO AS 'GLAZING', AS IF IT WERE A SPECIAL TECHNIQUE – IN FACT, IT IS THE NORMAL WAY OF WORKING WITH THIS MEDIUM.

SEE ALSO

Wet-on-dry, pages 42–43

Glazing is a technique that was perfected by the early painters using oils. They would lay thin skins of transparent pigment one over the other to create colours of incredible richness and luminosity.

Watercolour is noted for its transparency and this makes it highly suited to glazing. Layers of transparent washes allow the white paper underneath to 'shine' through, and it's this that gives watercolour its characteristic luminosity. The effects created by the technique are quite different than those of colour applied opaquely, because light seems to reflect through each layer, creating the illusion that the painting is almost lit from within.

As well as traditional watercolour, acrylic paint is perfectly suited to the glazing technique. When glazing, each layer must be thoroughly dry before the next one is applied and acrylic has the advantage of drying fast.

Special media are sold for acrylic glazing – available in both gloss and matt – and these can be used either alone or in conjunction with water. A whole painting can be built up layer by layer in this way.

SUGGESTED APPLICATIONS

• Apply glazes wherever you want to build up colour and tone without obscuring the brightness of the paper underneath.
• Use to 'mix' colour directly on the paper – think of your glazes as a tissue paper collage where each new layer alters the colour of the underlying layer.

LAYERING COLOUR
Dancer by Ann Smith
Smith's lovely image owes much of its impact to the combination of wet-in-wet and overlays of glazed colour, which give depth to each area. It was begun more or less as an abstract, with splashes of transparent colour, but once the figure of the dancer began to emerge the artist 'drew in' her face and arms more carefully.

GLAZING OVER IMPASTO

Thin glazes can also be laid over an area of thick paint ('impasto') to great effect. The glaze will tend to slide off the raised areas and sink into the lower ones – a useful technique for suggesting textures, such as those of weathered stones or tree bark.

COLOUR PREPARATION
Transparency is the key characteristic to bear in mind when glazing so it is advisable to do some colour preparation on a separate piece of paper before starting a painting. Judge the transparency of your chosen colours by layering them over one another in a test strip.

WORKING LIGHT TO DARK

1 Glazing relies on the application of successive layers of watercolour to develop colour, tone and intensity. It should be done slowly, and gradual changes made until the desired effect is achieved. A smooth, cold-pressed paper will hold many layers of paint satisfactorily but a soft brush and a light hand is required to avoid disturbing previous layers of paint. It is important to work from light to dark so that the highlights and lightest tones are first established.

2 Colour is built up on the paper by applying thin washes of transparent colour. Here, layers of blue and yellow are applied to a green leaf until the desired tonal values of green are reached.

STAINING PIGMENTS

3 Another property which may be considered when glazing is staining quality. Synthetically produced dye pigments such as Quinacridones will generally stain the paper while those made from metallic oxides and salts such as the Cadmiums will sit in a layer on the surface. Using diluted staining pigments initially may allow more layers to be added as they are less likely to be removed by subsequent applications.

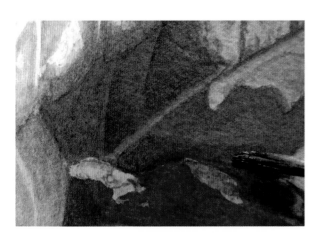

4 The shadowy areas between the leaves and on the darker coloured leaves are painted by layering blue and violet over maroon, gold and yellow to produce rich, dark areas of colour.

ACHIEVING MUTED TONES

5 Applying light, bright layers initially allowed the white paper to glow through the paint producing vibrant colours, which add a jewel-like quality to the subject. Muted tones can be achieved by glazing complementary colours over one another, such as yellow over violet, or by layering more opaque colours for a flatter finish.

BACK RUNS AND BLOSSOMS

BACK RUNS FORM NATURALLY AND ARE A QUIRKY CHARACTERISTIC OF THE WATERCOLOUR MEDIUM. BOTH A NUISANCE AND A DELIGHT TO PAINTERS, THEY CAN BE TREATED AS MISTAKES OR EXPLOITED TO THE ARTIST'S ADVANTAGE.

If you lay a wash and apply more colour into it before it is completely dry, the chances are that the new paint will seep into the old, creating strangely shaped blotches with hard, jagged edges. These 'back runs' are also sometimes called 'cauliflowers' or 'blossoms' because of their organic, flower-like appearance. They do not always occur, however; the more absorbent or rough-textured papers are less conducive to the formation of back runs than smoother, highly sized ones.

If you don't want a back run and one does form, the only remedy is to wash off the entire area and start again. With practice it is possible to avoid them completely. However, many watercolour painters create back runs deliberately, both in large areas such as skies or water, or in small ones such as the petals of flowers, since the effects they create are unlike those achieved by conventional brushwork. For example, a realistic approximation of reflections in gently moving water can be achieved by lightly working wet colour or clear water into a still-damp wash. The paint or water will flow outwards, giving an area of soft colour with the irregular, jagged outlines so typical of reflections.

SUGGESTED APPLICATIONS

• Use to suggest organic forms, such as blocks of foliage, flower shapes or cumulus clouds.
• Back runs also work well for irregular, hard-edges shapes, such as reflections in water.

ABSTRACT SHAPES
Elementals No. 18
by David Castle
Based on a geometric framework, each shape is measured and drawn with a pencil and ruler, then painted wet-on-dry. Next, varying amounts of paint and water were dropped in to form 'blooms' or back runs. While still wet, additional colours were dropped in to give more depth and interest.

APPLYING INITIAL WASHES
1 The artist drops Rose Madder, Dioxazine Violet, Naples Yellow and Winsor Blue onto wet paper and allows the colours to blend.

WHEN TO ADD PAINT

It takes a little practice to be able to judge how wet or dry the first wash should be before adding more paint or water to create a back run. As a general guide, if there is still a sheen on the wash it is too wet and the colours will merge together without forming a back run, as they do when working wet-in-wet.

DROPPING IN WATER AND COLOUR

2 While the colour is still wet, the artist drops clear water from a clean brush into the paint. The water carries the pigment to the edge of the droplet as it continues to spread.

GRANULATION

Certain colours have a tendency to granulate – separate on the paper to create a spotty, grainy texture, rather like the mottling you might see in certain kinds of stone. Using these pigments when creating back runs can add further surface interest and texture.

3 Continuing the method, the artist drops some Dioxazine Violet into the still-damp Rose Madder and the Winsor Blue, and then sits back and watches the paint spread.

4 Once dry, the painting shows the blossoms and florets with the concentration of pigment around the edges. Smaller splashes have made smaller blossoms.

SEE ALSO

Wet-in-wet, pages 44–45
Hard edges, pages 48–49
Granulation, pages 60–61

FEATHERING AND MOTTLING

BOTH FEATHERING AND MOTTLING EXPLOIT WATERCOLOUR'S INHERENT TENDENCY TO BLEED IF THE SURROUNDING SURFACE IS DAMP – BUT WITH DIFFERENT RESULTS.

Working wet-in-wet is a classic watercolour technique but the feathering and mottling methods take this one step further. Instead of washing an entire area with water or paint and allowing the next wash to flow into it before the first wash is dry, these two techniques wet only certain areas, so the paint bleeds in a much more controlled way only where the artist wants it to.

In the case of feathering, bands of clean water are painted across a dry surface – either unpainted paper or a dry wash; then, while these are still wet, bands of a coloured wash are laid at right angles across the water. The paint bleeds with a feather-like effect where it touches the water, but dries in hard-edged lines in the gaps in between. This can be a useful technique for rendering linear patterns, such as reflections in water.

The mottling technique is similar, except that the water is added afterwards, flicked onto the paint while it is still wet. Because the water is applied in a more random way, the final result is less predictable. But, as with all watercolour techniques, unpredictability is part of the charm and fascination of the medium.

SUGGESTED APPLICATIONS
• Use to convey a stand of pine trees or tracery of branches in a forest canopy.
• Feathering can also work well for reflections in water.
• Mottling is an immensely useful technique for painting woodland trees and branches. It seems to present the labyrinth of tiny twigs exactly as they appear. It would be impossible to paint every little mark, but this rapidly creates instant tree texture.

MOTTLED BRANCHES
Country Lane by Joe Dowden
In this painting (far left), the artist demonstrates a deft application of the mottling technique. Rather than attempting to paint every branch in a tight and controlled way, he merely suggests the delicate tracery. The result is loose and lively. The soft, feathery shapes are counterbalanced by the bold, hard-edged shadows in the water below.

SOFTENED COLOUR
Spring Ballet by Jan Hart
Washes of delicate colour have been loosely applied to the foliage of the tree in the foreground (left), leaving large areas white. A few quick lines have been sketched in for the framework of branches and allowed to bleed in parts to soften them. The whole effect is one of light and movement.

2 While still wet, parallel lines of colour are applied at right angles to the strokes of water. As the lines of paint pass across the lines of water, they diffuse sideways, creating a feather-like effect.

FEATHERING

1 First, several strokes of water are dragged loosely across the paper. The strokes are spaced out so that there are gaps between them. Pressing too hard will make the water soak into the paper, so care is needed. The brush needs to be dragged gently but firmly along the surface so that the tooth of the paper 'grabs' some of the moisture, while many of the tiny pits and dimples in the surface texture are left dry.

SEE ALSO

Wet-in-wet, pages 44–45
Back runs and blossoms, pages 52–53
Spraying water, pages 58–59
Spattering, pages 84–85

MOTTLING

1 The artist paints squiggly lines in a strong colour.

CRISS-CROSS FEATHERING

You can vary the feathering technique by applying the strokes of water loosely at different angles, still leaving plenty of dry paper, to achieve a more random effect.

2 Before the lines of paint are dry, he spatters clean water over them by firmly tapping it over his hand and fingers, and letting droplets fly off onto the paper. Where the water hits the paint, the colour diffuses outwards.

TIPS: MIXING COLOUR

• When feathering, you need to have your colours mixed in sufficient quantity before you begin because the paint needs to be applied quickly before the water dries, or it will not 'feather'.

• It's important to use a wet, free-flowing mix and rich colour for this technique. This will ensure that the original framework of lines remains strong, and does not lose its impact where it is diffused by water.

LIFTING OUT

LIFTING OUT IS NOT ONLY A METHOD OF CORRECTION THAT ALLOWS THE ARTIST TO REMOVE EXCESS COLOUR FROM PARTS OF A PAINTING, BUT IS ALSO A USEFUL AND ADAPTABLE WATERCOLOUR TECHNIQUE IN ITS OWN RIGHT.

SEE ALSO

Reserving highlights, pages 74–75
Sponging, pages 82–83
Correcting mistakes, pages 102–103
Perspective, pages 126–127

A number of different tools may be used to lift out paint. For instance, the effect of streaked wind clouds in a blue sky is quickly and easily created by laying a blue wash and wiping a dry sponge, paintbrush or paper towel across it while it is still wet. The white tops of cumulus clouds can be suggested by dabbing the wet paint with a sponge or some blotting paper.

Another useful aid to lifting out is gum arabic, which binds watercolour pigments and is also used as a medium. Add it in small quantities to the colour you intend to remove partially.

Paint can also be lifted out when dry by using a dampened sponge or other such tool, but the success of the method depends both on the colour to be lifted and the type of paper used. Certain colours, such as Sap Green and Phthalocyanine Blue, act rather like dyes, staining the paper, while some papers absorb the paint, making it hard to move it around. Heavier-weight cold-pressed and rough papers are more robust and can take more punishment, and thus are excellent for lifting out in this way.

SUGGESTED APPLICATIONS
• Use to soften edges, diffuse and modify colour, and create those highlights that cannot be reserved.
• Use to blur background areas so that they appear to recede, thus creating the illusion of three-dimensional depth (see Spatial Depth, pages 128–129).

INITIAL LIFTING OUT
1 A loose, uneven wash is laid down for the sky. While the paint is still wet, cloud shapes are lifted out by pressing firmly with paper towel.

CHOOSING TOOLS

When lifting out large areas of dry paint, a dampened sponge works well. However, for smaller areas or more intricate work, a more precise tool is needed. Choose your tool for lifting off with your subject in mind.

• A clean No.6 brush can be used to lift out lines and here, it is used to suggest the shape of bricks in a wall.

• Use a natural sponge and wipe downwards with a strong movement to make rays of light.

• A clean, wet brush is used to lift off paint and create soft highlights.

2 By varying the pressure applied, different amounts of colour can be removed. The paper towel can also be rolled to a point to lift out fine detail, as shown here.

CREATING TONE AND FORM

3 A pale wash is applied for the sea. A piece of paper towel is then dragged across the damp wash to create varying bands of tone and colour. The paint is left to dry.

4 The distant headlands are painted in a grey-blue wash and the hills in the foreground in a deep green. Paper towel is again used to blot up some of the colour in the foreground to suggest forms in the landscape.

6 By restricting the palette to sombre blues and greens, the artist has given the painting an overall unity. When seen as a whole, it does not lack drama however, due to the powerful contrasts in tone and texture that lifting out can produce.

5 While the paint is still damp, a clean, dry brush is used to lift out colour in the middle distance to suggest a flat area between the hills.

SPRAYING WATER

THIS TECHNIQUE IS SIMILAR TO DROPPING IN CLEAR WATER TO CREATE BACK RUNS, BUT INVOLVES USING A SPRAY BOTTLE OR DIFFUSER TO ACHIEVE A MUCH MORE SUBTLE SPECKLED EFFECT.

Watercolour is a highly flexible medium, allowing the artist to create a wide range of effects. All depend on the way in which the paint interacts with water – as well as how much or how little water is involved. Spraying a wash with water is another way of manipulating the medium and taking advantage of its natural tendency to spread when wet. However, because the drops of water are small the effect is much more understated than with, say, back runs or other similar techniques – it is effectively a way of distressing the surface to produce a texture.

WHEN TO SPRAY

Timing is crucial with this technique – spray when the paint is still damp but has lost its surface sheen. If you spray while the area is still too wet, the water droplets will merge into the paint without leaving a mark.

LAYING WASHES
1 Working wet-in-wet, the artist adds washes of several different colours to the paper and lets the colours blend together.

SPRAYING THE DAMP PAINT
2 While the paint is still damp, water is sprayed onto it in short bursts from a bottle.

3 When the paint is dry, a random pattern of tiny watermarks is visible.

GRANULATION

ALTHOUGH NOT STRICTLY A TECHNIQUE IN ITS OWN RIGHT BUT PART OF THE BEHAVIOUR OF CERTAIN COLOURS, GRANULATION CAN NEVERTHELESS BE USED BY THE WATERCOLOUR ARTIST TO GREAT EFFECT.

With some colours, pigment particles attract each other to produce a grainy effect called granulation. What may look like an alarming mistake to a novice – and one that must be corrected immediately – is appreciated by the more experienced painter as one of the delights unique to this medium, to be preserved and enjoyed. The texture produced by granulation is often very beautiful and can enhance a painting.

Granulating colours include several of the blues – Ultramarine, Cobalt, Manganese and Cerulean – as well as Viridian, Raw Sienna and Raw Umber. If the name on the label is followed by the word 'hue', that colour may not granulate as well.

As an experiment that will produce an interesting two-tone texture, a granulating colour may be mixed with one that does not granulate well, for example, granulating Manganese Blue with non-granulating Alizarin Crimson.

SUGGESTED APPLICATIONS
• Exploit granulation to convey organic textures, such as those of masonry or stone.
• Use areas of granulation as a counterpoint and contrast with flat paint.

EXPLOITING DIFFERENT TECHNIQUES
Brittany Skyline by Roger Pickett
To build up the textures, Pickett has given himself a start by working on rough paper. The foreground was worked over a high-toned wash, and when dry, more paint was applied, mixed with granulating fluid, and the board was tilted to channel the granulation in various directions. Darker details were added first with a brush and then a sharpened twig, used to draw lines into the wet paint.

GRANULATION FLUID

Granulation fluid is a watercolour medium developed to make all colours granulate, if wished. It may be used straight or diluted with water, then mixed with the paint.

BRUSHING IN THE FIRST WASHES
1 The artist starts by brushing in a pool of Alizarin Crimson, followed by an overlapping pool of Manganese Blue (right).

GRANULATING COLOURS

This selection of granulating paints shows how the pigments settle on the watercolour paper. Don't be alarmed by this uneven appearance; it is normal and can be used to great effect in your painting.

YELLOW OCHRE   **VIRIDIAN GREEN**

CERULEAN BLUE

APPLYING A GRANULATING MIX
2 He then flows in an Alizarin-Manganese mix in the middle.

CHOOSING PAPER

For the best effect and maximum granulation, use a rough paper.

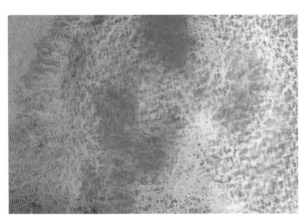

3 When the paint is dry, the effect is clearly visible. The Alizarin to the left has not granulated but the mixed violet in the middle and the Manganese to the right have clearly granulated, producing that distinctive texture.

INCREASING GRANULATION

The amount of granulation you can expect to see varies according to the texture of the paper, the amount (and type) of water used and the nature of the pigment itself. Although some pigments granulate on smooth, hot-pressed papers, the effect is increased if you use textured paper, as shown here. Mixing a particular colour with distilled water can also increase its granulation.

ON 250GSM COLD-PRESSED WATERCOLOUR PAPER

ON HANDMADE WATERCOLOUR PAPER

COBALT BLUE

LUNAR BLACK

WITH DISTILLED WATER

WITH GRANULATING MEDIUM

COBALT BLUE

LUNAR BLACK

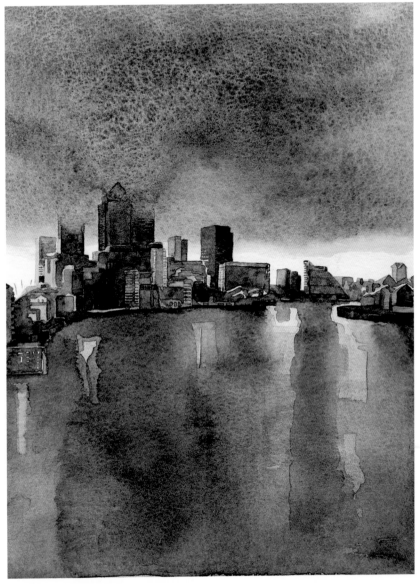

EXPLOITING GRANULATION

The Sky and the Water by Moira Clinch

In this wonderfully atmospheric painting, granulation has been deliberately induced in the sky area so that it has an almost solid presence. The water has been treated more smoothly, with carefully reserved highlights linking it to the sky and buildings above.

SEE ALSO

Back runs and blossoms, pages 52–53
Feathering and mottling, pages 54–55
Running in, pages 62–63
Spattering, pages 84–85

RUNNING IN

THIS IS A SIMILAR TECHNIQUE TO
CREATING BACK RUNS, BUT THIS TIME
THE BOARD IS TILTED TO ALLOW
GRAVITY TO ACT ON THE PAINT.

The difference between back runs and running in is that in the case of back runs the wet paint is allowed to spread in whatever direction it naturally wants to go, carrying a 'tidemark' of pigment with it; with running in, the direction in which the water or wet paint runs is controlled by lifting the board so that it runs downwards.

Running in has a limited number of applications compared with other watercolour techniques, but it's worth knowing nevertheless – watercolour is an incredibly flexible medium, offering a wider range of effects than perhaps any other painting medium, so it's good to be aware of every option. If this technique is controlled carefully and the wetness of the wash judged correctly when the water is dropped in, the final effect can be subtle and pleasing.

The soft, vertical forms created by running in are suggestive of reflections in water, and could also be used to convey wet surfaces such as pavements. Carefully controlled, it could express the highlights on a shiny, cylindrical object.

SUGGESTED APPLICATIONS
• Use the running-in technique wherever you want soft, vertical forms, for example, to convey reflections in water or the highlights on straight-sided, cylindrical objects such as vases.

LAYING A WASH
1 A flat wash is laid down on the paper.

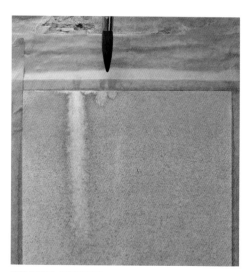

RUNNING IN WATER
2 While the wash is still wet, the board is held upright and a brush holding clean water is touched to the top. The water runs down, carrying the pigment with it.

FLOWING IN COLOUR
Broad Sunlit River by Joe Francis Dowden
To convey the reflections of the trees in the water, the artist needed to flow colour, rather than water, into the painted surface of the river. Working wet-in-wet and using Cadmium Lemon, Burnt Sienna, Payne's Grey and other pigments, he allowed the lines of colour to diffuse and spread to create the blurry reflections.

3 More drops of clear water are touched to the top of the still-wet paint.

4 After the paint has dried, soft-edged passages of lighter colour are left within the wash.

DROPPING IN COLOUR

Drop a colour into a wet area and allow it to react as its nature determines. It may diffuse, feather, bleed, creep, drop or shoot, depending on the introduced pigment and the density of the receiving wash. In these examples, Carbazole Violet (Dioxazine), a concentrated, dark organic pigment, receives inorganic and organic pigments very differently. Because of this unpredictability, experiment first on scrap paper before committing dropped-in colour to your painting.

NICKEL AZO
If Nickel Azo is introduced into a lighter-weight wash, it shoots wildly. If the receiving wash is not wet enough, it drops to the paper.

COBALT VIOLET
This granulating pigment dives for the paper.

CADMIUM ORANGE
This heavy pigment dives in and spreads out into the lower layers of the wash, altering the colour.

PERYLENE MAROON
This pigment appears to fuse with the wash it enters.

ULTRAMARINE BLUE
This pigment displays a ghostly, soft infiltration.

QUINACRIDONE GOLD
This displays a feathery edge in the Carbazole wash.

RUNNING IN COLOUR

Instead of running in clear water, you could run in a wash of another colour, wet-in-wet, tilting the board so that the colour runs downwards and diffuses into the underlying wash.

SEE ALSO

Back runs and blossoms, pages 52–53
Feathering and mottling, pages 54–55

BRUSHWORK

KNOWING WHICH BRUSH TO CHOOSE FOR THE TASK IN HAND, AND HOW TO HANDLE IT, CAN MAKE THE WATERCOLOURIST'S JOB THAT MUCH EASIER – AND ENSURE GREATER SUCCESS IN THE FINISHED WORK.

There's a common belief that brushwork is important only in oil painting. Watercolours are painted in gentle, flat washes, aren't they, with no obvious brushmarks? Well, yes and no. You can paint entirely in washes, as with wet-in-wet, where you certainly can't see any marks. But the marks a brush makes can be quite expressive, so it seems a pity not to make use of this resource. Some watercolourists build entire paintings by drawing with their brushes, using few, if any, flat washes, as in classical Chinese painting with its almost calligraphic brushstrokes.

Watercolour brushes come in all shapes and sizes and it is worth exploring the wide variety available, as well as learning what kinds of marks individual brushes can make. Wide, flat brushes are designed to make wide, flat marks, and are good for laying washes. Round brushes are perhaps more versatile, depending on how they are used. A fine to medium round brush can make broader marks if you apply more pressure, whereas if only the point is lightly touched to the paper, a fine line will be produced.

Always have more than one brush on hand, and when making marks be sensitive to what you are trying to convey – short, criss-crossing marks can suggest the texture of foliage; fine, zig-zagging strokes are perfect for the reflections of trees in water.

SUGGESTED APPLICATIONS

• Let the shape of the brushmarks suggest their use. For example, dry-brush done with a flat brush creates a texture reminiscent of the textured surfaces of wood and rocks. 'Dancing' brushstrokes are good for foliage and vegetation.

RESPONDING TO THE SUBJECT
Matador by Mary Ann Rogers
This painting demonstrates the artist's superb command of the watercolour medium. Her sensitivity to her subject is seen in the way in which she has varied her brushstrokes in response to the patterning and movement of the bird's plumage.

'DANCING' BRUSHSTROKES

1 To create dancing brushstrokes with a flat brush, the loaded brush is applied, edge-on, to the paper and swept either up or downwards.

2 Though the brushstrokes are not as varied in width, a round brush makes very consistent, narrow, pointed 'dancing' linework.

DRY-BRUSH

1 To work the dry-brush technique with a flat brush, a very lightly loaded brush is held nearly parallel to the surface and moved quickly across the paper. Some paint is released onto the raised areas, creating a scumbled effect.

2 A round brush works as well as a flat one for dry-brush.

GRIP AND PRESSURE

How you hold your brush, and the pressure you exert, can alter your brushstrokes.

- Brush held almost upright; a light stroke made with tip

- Brush slanted, with pressure reduced at the end of the stroke

- Brush held near the top, with light pressure

- Brush twisted in mid-stroke

Rounded marks for the wing feathers

Long, vertical strokes for the head feathers

Short, straight strokes for the breast feathers

Thin lines for the feathers near the feet

TWO-COLOUR STROKES

This technique is possible only with a flat brush. Load one edge of a flat brush with one colour, then load the other edge with a different colour, and make dancing brushstrokes.

CONVEYING SUBJECTS

Sketchbook Study by David Boys
Here the artist has developed a 'language' of brushmarks to describe this bird's feathers. The marks follow the direction of the feathers, and vary in shape and in length from long to short – short, curling brushmarks convey the patterns on the long feathers, and dots and dashes the shorter breast feathers.

BRUSH DRAWING

DRAWING WITH A BRUSH IS AN EXCELLENT WAY TO LOOSEN YOUR TECHNIQUE, REQUIRING NO UNDERDRAWING IN PENCIL.

Opaque water-based paints are not suitable for brush drawing because they produce too solid a mark – the marks and lines you make must be fluid and must flow easily from brush to paper, so use ordinary watercolour, watercolour ink or even acrylic paint, diluted with water to a wash.

With practice you will learn how much pressure to apply to your brush to make the line thicker, thinner, lighter or darker. Light pressure with the tip of a medium-sized, pointed brush will give a precise, delicate line. A little more pressure will thicken the line, while increasing it still further will produce a shaped brushmark rather than a line. It is even possible to produce a line of great sensitivity that is thick in places and thin in others, a highly pleasing effect.

SUGGESTED APPLICATIONS
• Brush drawing is especially useful whenever you want your work to appear free and spontaneous.
• The technique is also good for conveying movement in a variety of subject matter.

SPONTANEOUS DRAWING
Down to the Start by Jake Sutton
Drawing spontaneously with the brush is an excellent way to convey movement, which forms the main theme of this sparkling picture. Movement is expressed in every area, from the scribbled clouds to the blobs and splashes of paint used for awnings and foreground figures.

DRAWING IN THE OUTLINES
1 Using a fine brush and working on dry paper for a crisp effect, the artist draws in the main outlines of the bottles, making the lines in the foreground darker than those behind. The lines are then washed over with water to soften them – this will also allow the artist to erase and rework any errors. Loose washes of the same colour are applied within the outlines, and to the surrounding area.

ADDING DEFINITION
2 When the paint is slightly dry, washes of darker colours are applied to define the shapes of the bottles, and to add shadows and depth to the surrounding area.

3 White or pale patches are left unpainted, for highlights. The artist continues building up the picture in this way.

4 The finished painting has sufficient definition for the objects in it to be clearly recognizable, but the looseness of the technique ensures that the whole retains its impressionistic approach.

TIPS: DRAWING LINES

• Vary the weight of your lines to suggest three-dimensional form. Thin lines suggest delicacy and lightness, while thicker lines convey greater solidity and weight, as can be seen in the bottles here.

• Wherever the underpainting is still wet, any marks or lines you make will bleed so if you want crispness make sure that the underpainting is dry first.

SEE ALSO

Brushwork, pages 64–65

USING DIFFERENT BRUSHES

Mad March Hares by Julie Cassels
As well as applying different degrees of pressure to your brush to vary the lines and marks you make, try using a selection of brushes, including broad, flat-ended ones, and your mark-making repertoire will be almost endless. This will give a spontaneity and movement to your paintings.

CHINESE BRUSHES

In Chinese brush painting, brushmarks are pared down to a minimum to capture the essence of a subject. Here, the flower petals are achieved by applying heavy pressure.

DRY-BRUSH

THIS TECHNIQUE IS JUST WHAT ITS NAME IMPLIES – PAINTING WITH THE BARE MINIMUM OF PAINT ON THE BRUSH SO THAT THE COLOUR ONLY PARTIALLY COVERS THE PAPER.

The dry-brush method is one of the most common ways of creating texture and broken colour in watercolour. It needs practice: if there is too little paint, it will not cover the paper at all, but if there is too much, it will simply create a rather blotchy wash.

As a general principle, the technique should not be used all over a painting, since this can look monotonous. Texture-making methods work best in combination with others, such as flat or broken washes.

Opaque gouache and acrylic are also well suited to the dry-brush technique. In both cases the paint should be used with only just enough water to make it malleable – or even none at all. Cold-pressed or rough papers lend themselves best to this technique; as the dry paint is skimmed across the coarse surface, it adheres to the raised spots but does not sink into the indentations, automatically creating a textured effect.

SUGGESTED APPLICATIONS
• Use in landscapes for foliage and grass.
• Apply in seascapes to suggest the texture of the waves or highlights on the water.
• Use in portraits or animal painting to indicate the linear texture of hair or fur.

USING BODY COLOUR
Pensive by Tracy Hall
The artist has used a variation of the dry-brush method to build up the texture of the animal's fur. She began with a tiny brush and pure watercolour, and towards the end added opaque white, which dries the paint by giving it more substance.

ESTABLISHING THE MAIN AREAS

1 Having pressed out excess moisture from the brush, the artist drags grey-blue watercolour across the paper for the sea. Since the paint is fairly dry, it does not spread evenly over the paper like a fluid wash, but produces a patchy finish suggestive of sparkling water.

2 While this is drying, she adds washes for the sky and an uneven wash of light ochre for the beach.

WORKING THE FOREGROUND
3 Using a flat, broad brush and ochre, she begins to dry-brush the marram grass on the shore.

4 When the first layer of grass is dry, she builds up subsequent layers in the same way, dry-brushing progressively darker colours over the lighter tones. She also adds a small figure, partially hidden by the grass.

5 When the sea is completely dry, she dry-brushes streaks of Indigo mixed with Cerulean Blue over it. She also paints in the headland, overlaying a wash of grey-blue on top of the semi-dry sky so that the two blend a little to create a softer effect.

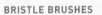

ADDING HIGHLIGHTS
6 The picture is completed with the addition of a little white gouache for extra highlights on the sea. Highlights are also scratched into the grass with a craft knife, and – as a final touch – the small figure of a dog running along the sand is placed in the middle ground.

BRISTLE BRUSHES

The best dry-brush effects are obtained with bristle, not soft sable or synthetic-hair, brushes (these are, in any case, quickly spoiled by such treatment).

SEE ALSO
Using salt, pages 88–89
Creating texture, pages 94–95

TONED GROUND

PRE-TINTING WATERCOLOUR PAPER TO CREATE A TONED GROUND OFFERS SEVERAL ADVANTAGES TO THE WATERCOLOUR ARTIST.

SEE ALSO

Stretching paper, page 27
Flat wash, pages 36–37
Wet-on-dry, pages 42–43

Although most watercolourists work on white paper, there are times when you might want to work on a lightly coloured ground. The advantages are two-fold. First, it helps you to achieve unity of colour because the ground shows through the applied colours to some extent, particularly if you leave small patches uncovered. Second, it allows you to build up deep colours with fewer washes, thus avoiding the risk of muddying. This is especially well suited to opaque gouache work where muddying occurs very easily.

It is possible to buy heavy coloured papers for watercolour work, but these may not always be easy to find, in which case you will need to colour your own paper. You do this by laying an overall wash of thinned acrylic, or an overall watercolour wash. For any but the heaviest weights of paper, it is necessary to stretch the paper first.

The main problem with pre-tinting is deciding what colour to use. Some artists like to paint a cool picture, such as a snow scene, on a warm, Yellow Ochre ground so that the blues, blue-whites and greys are heightened by small amounts of yellow showing through. Others prefer cool grounds for cool paintings and warm ground for warm ones. Think carefully about the overall colour key of your painting before pre-tinting; it can be helpful to try out one or two ground colours first.

SUGGESTED APPLICATIONS

• Apply a toned ground wherever you want to create a unified, coherent effect.
• A toned ground is also useful if you want to concentrate most of your marks in one part of the painting – the toned ground will 'fill' the rest of the space so that the picture still works as a whole, without looking unfinished.

TINTING THE PAPER

1 First, the artist lightly sketches in the subject matter. He then tints the paper with a wash of Raw Umber acrylic paint. The paint is initially applied with a brush and then rubbed with tissue to create a slightly uneven, patchy finish.

WORKING WET-IN-WET

2 When the initial wash is thoroughly dry, the artist re-wets the paper and begins to deepen the colour in parts. Re-wetting the paper allows the paint to spread so that no hard edges form and the effect remains soft and blurry.

3 Maintaining a limited palette and continuing to work wet-in-wet, the artist builds up the tones and paints in the softer details, such as the reflections of the pier supports.

WORKING WET-ON-DRY

4 Once the atmosphere and colour have been established, the painting is allowed to dry. Working wet-on-dry, crisper details can then be added.

5 Further details are added wet-on-dry, such as the building at the top right, the pier supports running across the top of the picture, the dark, wooden breakwaters and the birds in the sky.

6 The toned ground and the disciplined palette bring together all the elements of the picture, giving unity and coherence. The tones become deeper towards the foreground increasing the sense of space and light.

TIPS: PAINTING GROUNDS

• Before you begin your painting, experiment with different-coloured toned grounds on some spare paper. When the paint is dry, roughly brush on some of the colours you will be using in your final picture, to see what effect you get. Watercolour is translucent, so the toned ground will affect the colours applied on top.

• Remember that if you apply an overall toned ground, you will not be able to reserve highlights because there will be no white paper left.

LINE AND WASH

LINE AND WASH IS A TYPE OF VISUAL
SHORTHAND – COMBINING LINE
TO INDICATE FORM WITH COLOUR
FROM THE BRUSH IS A RAPID AND
ECONOMICAL WAY TO CONVEY
A GREAT DEAL OF INFORMATION.

This technique has a long history and is still much used today, particularly for illustrative work. Before the eighteenth century, it was used mainly to put pale, flat tints over pen drawings, a practice that itself continued the tradition of the pen-and-ink wash drawings often made by artists as preliminary studies for paintings.

The traditional method is to begin with a pen drawing, leave it to dry, and then lay in fluid, light colour with a brush. One of the difficulties of using this method is to integrate the drawing and the colour in such a way that the washes do not look like a 'colouring in' exercise, so it is often more satisfactory to develop both line and wash at the same time, beginning with some lines and colour and then adding to and strengthening both as necessary.

Alternatively, you can work 'back to front', as it were, laying down the washes first to establish the main tones and then drawing on top. In this case, you will need to begin with a light pencil sketch as a guideline.

The inks used may be waterproof or non-waterproof. Non-waterproof inks will run and add to the loose expressiveness of the medium. Loose-flowing lines and washes do not have to be completely precise.

SUGGESTED APPLICATIONS

• Line and wash is particularly well suited to small, delicate subjects, such as botanical plant drawings, or where you want to express precision of form, as with architectural subjects.
• The technique also works well for quick figure studies, where you want to convey a sense of movement.

KIEV

PODOL DISTRICT . KIEV

Ray Evans

ARCHITECTURAL SUBJECTS

Street in Kiev by Ray Evans
Line and wash is an excellent technique for architectural subjects, as can be seen here. The artist has used watercolour sparingly, reinforcing his fresh, clean washes with lively pen lines supplying the finer detail. Responding to different elements within the scene, he has varied his line accordingly – straight lines for the timber cladding, spidery lines for the branches and circles for the stones and pebbles in the walls and road surface – so that the line adds interest to the picture as well as providing information.

INITIAL LINEWORK

1 A few short strokes, lines and markings are made with an Indian ink pen, by first dipping it in the ink pot and then drawing directly on the paper.

LAYING WASHES

2 When the ink lines are dry, a loose wash is brushed over them. Waterproof ink, which does not run, has been used here.

3 The artist continues to build up the colour over the ink drawing. Even though the colour is quite intense it is transparent, allowing the linework to show through – this is the essence of line and wash.

TIPS: DRAWING LINES

• Tone can be built up by drawing numerous fine lines close together, in a technique known as 'hatching'. If the lines cross, it is referred to as 'cross-hatching'. The tone created by hatched lines can be supplemented with dark washes, perhaps for windows or doorways on a building.

• You need not limit yourself to a dip pen for drawing the lines. Many different instruments can be used, including ballpoint pens, or even an old broken twig dipped in ink to create scratchy lines with their own spontaneity.

LEAVING UNPAINTED AREAS

4 Some of the linework is left unpainted so that it remains sharp and focused. As with all art, the trick is knowing when to stop and not to overwork a piece – it can be a real advantage to stop short of completing a very detailed image.

TIPS: MAKING MARKS

• Before making marks on what will be the finished piece, 'warm up' by experimenting with the pen on another sheet of paper.

• Take care that large droplets of ink do not roll off the pen and make large blots on the image.

SEE ALSO

Brush drawing, pages 66–67

RESERVING HIGHLIGHTS

ALTHOUGH YOU CAN CREATE WHITE HIGHLIGHTS BY APPLYING OPAQUE WHITE PAINT, THE PUREST HIGHLIGHTS IN WATERCOLOUR WORK ARE MADE BY 'RESERVING' – THAT IS, LEAVING THE PAPER BARE.

RESERVING LARGE AREAS
Spanish Farm by Joe Francis Dowden
Space and brightness are vital in this stark, uncompromising Spanish highland. To retain the quality of sunlight falling on the white walls of the farm buildings, the artist reserved that part of the picture. Once he had established the colours and tones of the surrounding hills, he applied colour to the buildings.

The light reflecting off white paper is an integral part of watercolour painting, giving good watercolours their lovely, translucent quality. For this reason, the most effective way of creating pure, sparkling highlights is to reserve areas that are to be white by painting around them. This means that when you begin a painting, you must have a clear idea of where the highlights are to be, so some advance planning is necessary.

When you lay a wash around an area to be reserved, it will dry with a hard edge. This can be very effective but it may not be what you want, for example, on a rounded object such as a piece of fruit. In such cases, you can achieve a gentler transition by softening the edge with a brush, small sponge or cotton bud dipped in water.

Small highlights, such as the points of light in eyes or the tiny sparkles seen on sunlit, rippling water, which are virtually impossible to reserve because of their size, can be achieved either by masking or by applying white gouache as a final stage. Highlights can also be created by removing paint, by lifting out or scraping back.

SUGGESTED APPLICATIONS
• Use highlights to create tonal contrast and give the illusion of three-dimensional form.
• Reserve crisp highlights on shiny objects and softer highlights on more matt surfaces.

MAKING AN INITIAL SKETCH
1 The artist makes a preliminary drawing, lightly sketching in the shapes of the highlights so that they will be easy to reserve.

APPLYING THE WASHES
2 The highlight is to be an important feature of the painting, so the teapot is painted first. Because the pot has a reflective surface, the edges of the highlights are crisp, an effect the artist wants to exploit fully.

3 The background and the other objects are painted with all the highlights reserved as white paper or a pale colour. The artist now begins to build the darker tones.

4 The softer highlight on the spout of the teapot is made by reserving the lighter colour, that is, painting darker washes around the original light pinkish-brown.

SEE ALSO

Lifting out, pages 56–57
Scraping back, pages 76–77
Masking, pages 78–79
Body colour, pages 96–97

SOFT HIGHLIGHTS

To create a soft, coloured highlight, apply slightly diluted Chinese white or white gouache on top of the colour. The white will sink slightly into the colour below to produce a gentle, soft-edged highlight, perfect for matt surfaces.

COLOURED HIGHLIGHTS

Not all highlights are pure white; in paintings where all the tones are dark, too many whites could be over-emphatic. In this instance, you will need to wait until some colour has already been applied, and then either reserve areas of an initial pale wash or build up really dark tones around a later, mid-toned one. If you want to work wet-in-wet, you will have to wait until the initial wash has dried completely before re-wetting the paper.

1 Soft tones are built up, wet-in-wet, on an underwash of pale blue.

2 Crisper shapes are added wet-on-dry for definition and form.

SCRAPING BACK

SOMETIMES CALLED SGRAFFITO, THIS TECHNIQUE SIMPLY INVOLVES REMOVING DRY PAINT SO THAT THE WHITE PAPER IS REVEALED.

The scraping back method is most often used to create the kind of small, fine highlights that cannot be reserved, such as the light catching blades of grass in the foreground of a landscape, or the small points of light you might see on the surface of rippled water. It is a more satisfactory technique than opaque white applied with a brush, because this can look clumsy and, if laid over a dark colour, does not cover it very well.

Scraping is done with a sharp knife, such as a craft knife, or with a razor blade. For the finest lines, use the point of the knife, but avoid digging it into the paper. A more diffused highlight over a wider area can be made by scraping gently with the side of the

knife or with a razor blade, which will remove some of the paint but not all of it. The method should only be used in the final stages of a painting because it scuffs the paper and makes it impossible to apply more paint on top; in addition the paint must be completely dry.

The same technique can be used for gouache or acrylic, but it is essential that the surface is one that can withstand this treatment.

SUGGESTED APPLICATIONS
• Use for tiny highlights that cannot be achieved either by masking or reserving; for example, delicate surface textures, blades of grass or sparkles on water.

LAYING A WASH

1 Layers of watercolour are first built up in the usual way. This kind of light underpainting will allow for scraping back later.

IMPROVISING TOOLS

3 Other tools can be used for scraping back. Here, a credit card provides a useful edge for scraping away bands of just-damp colour.

SCRAPING BACK DAMP PAINT

2 Using a round-bladed craft knife, the artist scrapes away the plant stems. This is done while the paint is just damp so that it is easier to remove. Working in this way requires careful judgement. If the paint is too wet, the colour will simply flow back into the space it previously filled; the paper surface will also be wetter and so more easily torn. If the paint is left to dry completely, however, it can be more difficult to scrape away.

4 A fingernail provides another ready tool for scraping back.

ADDITIONAL HIGHLIGHTS

5 If more highlights are required, the surface may be gently rubbed with sandpaper. This must only be done when the paint is completely dry – sandpaper will rip the surface of damp paper.

6 To create shafts of light, the sandpaper can be folded to a knife-edge (below).

DRAWING WITH A BLADE

You can use the blade of a scalpel or craft knife like a pen or pencil to 'draw' linear highlights or texture, as on the inner surface of this mushroom – but take care to judge the wetness of the surface correctly before you start.

PAPER QUALITY

This method will not be successful unless you have a good-quality, reasonably heavy paper – it should be no lighter than 300gsm. On a flimsier paper, you could easily make holes or spoil the surface.

CHOOSING SCRAPING TOOLS

Almost anything sharp enough to scratch away the surface of the paint can be used for scraping back, but consider first the kind of shape you want to make and choose your tool accordingly. For example, sandpaper gives an overall sparkle or, folded and used on edge, it creates more concentrated linear highlights. Blades also produce linear highlights, while a credit card 'pulls back' colour for a more diffused area of brightness.

7 Translucent watercolour washes and scraped-back areas give the finished still life a luminous quality.

SEE ALSO

Reserving highlights, 74–75
Masking, 78–79

MASKING

THE TWO MAIN PURPOSES OF MASKING ARE TO CREATE HIGHLIGHTS BY RESERVING CERTAIN AREAS OF A PAINTING, AND TO PROTECT ONE PART OF A PICTURE WHILE YOU WORK ON ANOTHER.

SEE ALSO
Wax resist, pages 80–81
Reserving highlights, pages 74–75
Scraping back, pages 76–77

If over-used, masking can detract from the spontaneity that we associate with watercolour, but it is a method that can be used creatively, giving exciting effects that cannot be obtained by using the more classic watercolour techniques. Liquid masking fluid or masking tape may be used.

The liquid is applied with a brush and comes in two forms. One has a slight yellow tint, allowing you to see the brushstrokes as you apply them. The disadvantage is that the yellow patches are visible as you paint and tend to give a false idea of the colour values. There is also a colourless type, which does not distort colour perception but can be hard to see. Fluid-filled pens are also available, allowing you to 'draw' with the fluid.

Once the fluid is completely dry, washes are painted over it. When the paint is dry, the mask is removed by gently rubbing with a finger or an eraser. The beauty of liquid mask is that it is a form of painting in negative – the brushstrokes you use can be as varied in shape as you like, and you can create lovely effects by using thick and thin lines, splodges and little dots.

Sometimes a painting needs to be approached methodically and dealt with in separate parts, and this is where the second main function of masking comes in. Liquid mask or masking tape (ideal for straight lines) can be used as a temporary stop for certain areas of the painting. Covering the whole area of the building with liquid mask or putting strips of masking tape along the edges will allow you to paint freely without the constant worry of paint spilling over to spoil the sharp, clean lines. Once the background is finished, the mask can be removed, and the rest of the painting carried out as a separate stage. It may be mechanical, but it is a liberating method for anyone who wishes to have complete control over paint.

SUGGESTED APPLICATIONS
• Reserve small, intricate highlights with liquid mask, for example a pattern of leaves and twigs catching the sunlight in a woodland scene.
• Use to protect one area of a picture while painting freely on another.

APPLYING INITIAL COLOUR
1 Using a light pencil outline as a guide, the artist begins painting in the petals of the flowers with washes of blue and purple watercolour. She also washes Raw Umber and Burnt Sienna over the stems. Patches of deeper blue are applied for the sky. The paint is left to dry completely.

MASKING OUT
2 She then masks the flowers and stems with liquid mask and leaves it to dry.

PAINTING OVER THE MASK
3 The artist paints a green wash all over the flowers, using directional strokes for the grasses. The paint is left to dry, then a few more stems in the foreground are masked out with fluid.

4 When the second coat of mask is dry, she paints darker green over the grasses and on the trees in the background. All the paint is now left to dry fully before the masking is removed.

5 Final details, such as the orange hearts of the flowers, are added with a fine brush.

TIPS: BEST PRACTICE

• If the paper is too rough or too smooth, masking will either be impossible to remove or will spoil the paper – the best surface is a medium one (known as 'NOT' or cold-pressed).

• Rubbing the paintbrush in wet soap before dipping it in the fluid makes it easier to clean later. The brush should also be cleaned immediately after use.

6 Masking has allowed the artist to work in a spontaneous way, and has produced an effect impossible with any other technique. When the mask is removed the results can be a little unpredictable – but any 'happy accidents' become key elements of the style.

WAX RESIST

THIS SIMPLE TECHNIQUE, BASED ON
THE ANTIPATHY BETWEEN OIL AND
WATER, CAN YIELD MAGICAL RESULTS.

Wax resist is a valuable addition to the
watercolourist's repertoire and involves
deliberately repelling paint from certain
areas of the paper while allowing it to settle
on others. If you draw over paper with wax
or an oily medium and then overlay this with
watercolour, the paint will slide off the
waxed or greasy areas. You can use either
an ordinary household candle or inexpensive
wax crayons. The British sculptor, Henry
Moore (1898–1986), also a draughtsman

of great imagination, used crayons and
watercolour for his series of drawings
of sleeping figures in the London
Underground during World War II.

The wax underdrawing can be as simple
or as complex as you like. You can suggest
a hint of pattern on wallpaper in a portrait
by means of a few lines, dots or blobs
made with a candle, or create an intricate
drawing using crayons with sharp points.

Wax beneath watercolour gives a
delightfully unpredictable speckled effect
which varies according to the pressure
you apply and the type of paper you use.
It is one of the best methods for imitating
natural textures, such as those of rocks,
cliffs or tree trunks.

SUGGESTED APPLICATIONS
• Use to create natural patterns and
textures, such as the bark of trees, dappled
sunlight or light through foliage.

APPLYING WAX AND OIL PASTEL
1 Having first lightly pencilled in the outlines of
the figures, the artist roughly scribbles over the
sunlit background and trees using a white wax
candle and green and yellow oil pastels.

PAINTING OVER THE RESIST
2 Dark shades of watercolour are then flooded
over the whole area. The waxy parts reject the
watercolour, but where there are tiny gaps in the
waxy surface the colour adheres, creating broken
shapes and a speckled effect that is characteristic
of the wax-resist technique.

FOAMING SEAS
Headland by Charles Knight RWS, ROI
Wax-resist techniques are used to create the frothy
waves in this picture which create a feeling of
movement and add drama to the composition.

3 It is difficult to achieve even coverage of the surface using a waxy medium, as seen here in close-up. However, the relative unpredictability of this technique is part of its charm, and adds valuable surface texture to the finished painting.

ADDING DEFINITION
4 When the initial washes are dry, additional tones are added to define the forms without overworking them.

5 The finished piece shows just how effective the wax-resist technique can be. The sunlit background and the shadowy forms in the foreground are suggested with just enough tone and detail in the lightest, most impressionistic way. The trick here, as always, is knowing when to stop, to avoid overworking and ruining the painting. Notice, too, the clever contrast between the bright, acid tones of the background and the cooler, deeper tones of the figures.

SEE ALSO
Masking, pages 78–79
Creating texture, pages 94–95

SPONGING

DABBING PAINT ONTO PAPER
WITH A SPONGE GIVES AN
ATTRACTIVE, MOTTLED EFFECT,
AND IS AN EXCELLENT WAY TO
DESCRIBE TEXTURE.

A sponge is an important part of the artist's toolkit. It can be used both to blot up excess colour, and also to apply colour when a textured effect is required. It can even be used to apply overall washes. Small artists' sponges are available, but you can improvise and cut a piece off a larger sponge.

Use a different sponge for different colours (or wash your sponge out thoroughly between applications). Where you want a drier application, it's easy to reduce the amount of paint you are applying simply by squeezing the sponge slightly to expel the excess. By applying denser paint in shadowed areas, you can suggest form as well as texture. If you've used too much paint – perhaps obscuring the highlights – remove some by dipping the sponge in clean water, squeezing out the surplus and dabbing back into the paint. You can do this even when the paint is dry.

There is no reason why whole paintings should not be worked using this method, but sponging does have its limitations. The marks made by a sponge are not precise enough for intricate work or fine detail, so in the later stages of a painting brushes are usually brought into play to create fine lines and details.

SUGGESTED APPLICATIONS

• Sponging is a useful way of creating a large mass of texture, for example, to simulate a profusion of ragged plants in a garden, undergrowth in the wild or perhaps the masonry in an old building or the rough appearance of rocky crags.

INITIAL SPONGING
1 The artist begins by sponging on yellow, orange and green for the sunlit areas of the foliage. To preserve the crispness of the marks and to prevent them spreading and softening, he sponges onto dry paper. He continues to add colour until the desired shape for the canopy of each tree is achieved. The paint is left to dry so that there is no muddying of subsequent colours.

VARYING THE TONES
2 The trunks and branches are painted in, using a brush. A loose band of colour is added along the bottom to indicate the ground. Darker, cooler tones are added with a sponge to indicate the shadowed foliage, and left to dry slightly.

CREATING TEXTURE
Summer Walk Unknown artist
The irregular texture of a natural sponge has been employed to make broad soft washes instead of using a brush and to create a broken, speckled texture for the foliage. A tracing paper stencil was used for the straight lines of the tree trunk.

3 A pale yellow wash is applied to the background, working from right to left and light to dark and allowing the wash to pick up some of the sponged colour in the foliage. This will have a softening effect on the sponging, so that the technique does not dominate the picture. The sponge is then used to apply a band of French Ultramarine across the foreground.

4 For extra definition, more dark tones are dabbed on with the sponge. Where the sponge is too unwieldy, a brush may be used to apply these darks.

ADDING HIGHLIGHTS

5 Finally white body colour is sponged on for the lightest foliage on the left.

WET OR DRY?

The crispest effects are achieved by sponging onto a dry surface. For a softer sponged effect, try dabbing the colour onto a slightly damp surface. Or work both wet and dry in different parts of the painting to create varying texture and definition.

6 The limited palette of yellow, orange, brown and blue gives the finished piece overall cohesion. Note, too, the careful balance between shadows on the left and highlights on the right, which avoids a confused mass of tones.

SEE ALSO

Spattering, pages 84–85

Using salt, pages 88–89

Stippling, pages 90–91

Scumbling, pages 92–93

Creating texture, pages 94–95

SPATTERING

SPRAYING OR FLICKING PAINT ONTO THE PAPER, ONCE REGARDED AS UNORTHODOX AND 'TRICKSY', IS NOW ACCEPTED BY MOST ARTISTS AS AN EXCELLENT MEANS OF ENLIVENING AN AREA OF FLAT COLOUR OR SUGGESTING TEXTURE.

Any medium can be used, but the paint must not be too thick or it will cling to the brush. To make a fine spatter, load a toothbrush with fairly thick paint, hold it horizontally above the paper, bristle side down, and run your index finger over the bristles. For a coarser effect, use a bristle brush, loaded with paint of the same consistency, and tap it sharply with the handle of another brush. The bristle brush method can also be used for watery paint, but will give much larger drops. Some artists like to use a paintbrush, flicking paint off it by tapping the metal part of the handle against the finger, to release a spray of paint.

The main problem with the method is judging the tone and depth of colour of the spattered paint against that of the colour beneath. If you apply dark paint – and thick watercolour will of necessity be quite dark – over a very pale tint, it may be too obtrusive. The best effects are created when the tonal values are close together.

SUGGESTED APPLICATIONS
• Apply to evoke natural textures, such as foliage, shingle or sand.

USE A MOUTH DIFFUSER

If you need to spatter one pale colour over another – for example, to express the texture of a pebbled or sandy beach, for which the technique is ideal – the best implement to use is a mouth diffuser of the kind sold for spraying fixative.

PRACTISE FIRST

Spattering is a somewhat unpredictable method and it takes some practice before you can be sure of the effect it will create, so it is wise to try it out on some spare paper first.

SUBTLE SUGGESTIONS
The Dublin Writers' Museum by Catherine Brennand
The artist has suggested the marble columns of this building through judicious applications of spattered paint, which are much more effective than any exact representation would be.

2 Tissue paper protects the foreground and sky from successive layers of spattering. More pigment is added at each stage to bring shadow and depth to the image.

BUILDING UP TEXTURE

1 Sap Green is gently spattered over a loose drawing of tree trunks, sections of which have been masked out to suggest dappled light.

3 The same green is brushed loosely over the foreground, with areas of blue and violet flooded in to suggest a carpet of bluebells. Salt is sprinkled in to add further texture.

SEE ALSO
Sponging, pages 82–83
Using salt, pages 88–89
Stippling, pages 90–91
Creating texture, pages 94–95

4 After all the spattered paint has dried, the tree trunks are painted with Burnt Umber and Sap Green.

BLOTS AND DROPS

FLICKING BLOTS OF PAINT ONTO DRY PAPER OR DROPPING SPOTS OF PAINT INTO A WET WASH ARE RELATIVELY RANDOM WAYS OF ADDING COLOUR, TEXTURE AND INTEREST – AND CAN PRODUCE SOME PLEASING AND SURPRISING RESULTS.

WORKING ON WET PAPER

Time to Crush by Jeanne Lamar
In her painting, the artist has dropped paint onto wet paper in places, producing subtle colour mixes and soft edges. Certain areas were then sharpened up, but with care taken to preserve the spontaneous effect.

Blot painting is a technique most often associated with monochrome ink drawing, but now that watercolours are available in liquid (ink) form this technique has become more popular with watercolour artists. The other reason for its inclusion is that it is an excellent way of loosening up technique and providing new visual ideas. Like back runs, blots are never entirely predictable, and the shapes they make will sometimes suggest a painting or a particular treatment of a subject quite unlike the one that was planned. Allowing the painting to evolve in this way can have a liberating effect and may suggest a new way of working in the future.

The shapes the blots make depend on the height from which they are dropped, the consistency of the paint or ink and the angle of the paper. Tilting the board will make the blot run downhill; flicking the paint or ink will create small spatters; wetting the paper will produce a diffused, soft-edged blot.

Dropping a blot onto the paper and then blowing it will send 'tendrils' of paint shooting out in various directions.

An associated technique exploits watercolour's tendency to spread when applied wet-in-wet. The method involves dropping small amounts of wet paint from a brush into a wet wash. The drops spread and feather out on their edges, rather like back runs, but because they are small and are applied in a more controlled way, the effect is different.

SUGGESTED APPLICATIONS
• Blots can be used to suggest the textures of a tree, flowers or pebbles.
• Blown 'tendrils' of colour may suggest stems and branches.
• Drops, applied to wet paint, are a good way of adding colour to textured foliage, or creating a marbled effect.

CHOOSING PIGMENTS

Different pigments have different qualities and thus behave in different ways. Some are opaque, some more translucent, some granulate, some dry flat. Experiment by dropping different colours into wet washes and observe how they interact, then choose the combinations that you like best and that produce the effects you want.

DROPPING COLOUR WET-ON-DRY
1 The artist flicks a loaded brush onto paper to produce these random paint blots.

DROPPING COLOUR WET-IN-WET

• A dense wash of a deep pink is brushed onto the paper. While the wash is still wet, Ultramarine is dropped in. The brush can be touched to the surface, or droplets can be allowed to fall off the brush from above. Larger droplets are made by using more paint, smaller ones by using less.

• As a variation, a wash of indigo was laid down and opaque colours were dropped onto it. Cadmium Lemon and Cobalt Turquoise Light are both lighter than indigo but because of their opacity they make an impression on the darker wash and push the indigo colour out to form darker ringlets.

BUILDING UP THE IMAGE
2 The blots suggest honesty seeds to the artist, so she builds up the picture by drawing in the paper-thin petals and stems of the plant, using a fine brush.

3 Washes of colour are added where necessary, and additional spots of colour are dabbed on with a finger.

4 The artist completes the work by adding in just enough definition to allow the image to be read figuratively, while taking care to retain the original spontaneity.

SEE ALSO
Back runs and blossoms, pages 52–53
Spattering, pages 84–85

USING SALT

THERE ARE NUMEROUS WAYS TO
BREAK UP AN AREA OF WATERCOLOUR
AND ADD TEXTURE. ONE OF THE MOST
INTERESTING AND UNEXPECTED IS TO
SPRINKLE A WET WASH WITH SALT.

SEE ALSO

Dry-brush, pages 68–69
Stippling, pages 90–91
Scumbling, pages 92–93

It is one of the paradoxes of painting that a large area of flat colour seldom appears as colourful, or as realistic, as one that is textured or broken up in some way. The Impressionists, working mainly in oils, discovered that they could best describe the shimmering effects of light on foliage or grass by placing small dabs of various greens, blues and yellows side by side instead of using just one green for each area. This technique can be adapted very successfully to watercolour, but there are many other ways to break up colour.

Dropping table or sea salt into the wet paint can produce some interesting textures. Being water-retentive, the grains of salt soak up the wetness of the paint from the immediate area, speeding up the drying process there. As the paint dries, little star shapes appear as the water floods out of the crystals and pushes the colour away to create feathered edges.

SUGGESTED APPLICATIONS

• The effects you achieve can be translated into different textures depending on the context in which they are used – snow, lichen, rocks, leaves, flowers and so on.

BACKGROUND INTEREST

Fleur de Fête by Katrina Small
In her painting, the artist has used salt spatter for the background alone. This contrasts nicely with the sharp delineation and careful blends used for the feet and sandals.

DIFFERENT-SIZED GRAINS

Salt grains of different sizes produce shapes and textures of different kinds. Experiment to see what you can create.

• Using larger salt grains produces more distinct star-like shapes with feathered edges.

• Smaller-grained salt produces a finer texture.

TIPS: CHOOSING A FINISH

• The wetness of the wash will determine the final result, so judge the wetness carefully to achieve the effect you want.

• Breaking up colour with salt is most effective in areas with an even finish, as this provides the greatest contrast.

CREATING PATTERNS WITH SALT
1 Initial washes establish the areas of sky, mountains and lake. While the washes are still wet, salt is sprinkled into selected areas – in this case, the sky, to create a cloud-like effect.

2 The salt is left to work. Meanwhile more colour is added wet-in-wet to achieve the required density in different parts of the picture, and the colours are allowed to bleed into each other.

3 The colours are deepened, still wet-in-wet, to strengthen the impression of the mountains and lake. Salt is sprinkled onto the lake to create a speckled pattern, like that of sparkling water.

VARYING THE WETNESS

One of the tricks in creating salt textures lies in judging the wetness of the paint, as this will affect the pattern you achieve, as shown in the examples below.

• Here salt is added to very wet paint, giving a softer and more diffuse effect.

• In this example, the salt is added after the paint has dried a little – still damp, but not running.

• Here the paint has almost dried; the effect is smaller and tighter.

STIPPLING

THIS METHOD OF APPLYING PAINT IN A SERIES OF SEPARATE, SMALL MARKS, USING THE TIP OF A BRUSH, PRODUCES A DISTINCT TEXTURE THAT IS QUITE DIFFERENT FROM OTHER TECHNIQUES. KNOWING HOW TO APPLY IT CAN ADD TO YOUR ABILITY TO CONVEY A VAST NUMBER OF POSSIBILITIES IN WATERCOLOUR.

STIPPLING SELECTED AREAS
Simple Pleasures by Denny Bond
The stippling in this picture has mainly been used for the foreground. Before applying colour, liquid masking was applied with a toothbrush to produce a ground texture, and then a further layer of stippled colour was added to achieve depth. The barn was painted in two successive dry washes.

Stippling was, and is, a technique favoured by painters of miniatures, and is seldom used for large paintings for obvious reasons. However, for anyone who enjoys small-scale work and the challenge of a slow and deliberate approach, it is an attractive method and can produce lovely results, quite unlike those of any other watercolour technique. It can be used to create texture, or as a method of blending colours and giving an area of colour greater depth.

If you are using the technique as a way of colour blending – similar to the pointillist method of the painter Seurat – success depends on the separateness of each dot or mark: The colours and tones should blend together in the viewer's eye rather than physically on the paper. As with all watercolour work, the stippled marks should be built up from light to dark, with highlights left white or only lightly covered so that the white ground shows through, while the dark areas are built up gradually with increasingly dense brushmarks. Highlights can also, of course, be added with body colour.

If your aim is to create an area of texture in a painting, the effect you achieve will depend on the brush you use, and on the wetness of the paint.

SUGGESTED APPLICATIONS
• Stippling can produce the perfect texture for many things – the rows of vines in a vineyard, the rough texture of ground, or the mottled face of a cliff, for example.

SEE ALSO

Using salt, pages 88–89
Scumbling, pages 92–93
Creating texture, 94–95

STIPPLING THE FIRST COLOUR

1 The artist loads an old sable brush with Cadmium Red and dots down colour onto the surface.

VARYING THE STIPPLE

2 Next, to create a contrasting stipple, he loads a large, flat hake brush liberally with a green mix. He shakes the brush to separate the fibres into clumps, then dabs it down repeatedly in a broad line to give roughly parallel lines of texture, rather like ploughed furrows in a field.

3 The marks from stippling create various possibilities – clumps of ferns or tyre tracks could be implied by these marks.

TIPS: VARYING CONSISTENCY

• The paint should have a creamy consistency when you are stippling – if it is too wet, the dots will merge or dissolve.

• The drier the paint, the more distinct a stippled pattern you will make.

• Once you feel reasonably confident with the technique, try varying the consistencies of the paints to produce distinct patterns.

MAKING RANDOM MARKS

Use the point of the brush to make random brushstrokes, allowing some of the marks to merge. Vary the marks depending on the kind of pattern or texture you want to create.

SCUMBLING

USUALLY DONE WITH A SHORT-HAIRED BRUSH (THE OLDER THE BETTER), SCUMBLING INVOLVES SCRUBBING DRY PAINT UNEVENLY OVER ANOTHER LAYER OF DRY COLOUR SO THAT THE FIRST LAYER SHOWS THROUGH IN PARTS.

SEE ALSO

Sponging, pages 82–83
Stippling, pages 90–91

This is one of the best-known of all techniques for creating texture and broken colour effects. Scumbling can give amazing richness to colours, creating a lovely glowing effect rather akin to that of a semi-transparent fabric with another, solidly coloured one beneath. There is no standard set of rules for the technique because it is fundamentally an improvisational one.

Scumbling is most frequently used in oil painting, but is in many ways even better suited to acrylic and gouache because they dry so much faster – the oil painter has to wait some time for the first layer to dry. The particular value of the method for gouache is that it allows colours to be overlaid without becoming muddy and dead-looking – always a danger with this medium.

Because of the relatively thin consistency of watercolour, the technique is less well suited to this medium than to gouache and acrylic. Whatever medium you are using, the trick is to apply dry paint as thickly as possible – if it is too wet, it will simply spread out across the paper. If you are scumbling with watercolour, it is more effective if you are using tubes, as you can then apply the paint undiluted, straight from the tube.

Use a rough paper, too, rather than a smooth, hot-pressed one. In the same way as the dry-brush technique, the dry, scrubbed-on paint will not be fluid enough to sink into the hollows but will adhere to the raised tooth, which will accentuate the scumbled texture.

SUGGESTED APPLICATIONS

• Use wherever you want to evoke a natural texture – for rocks, masonry, fur and so on.

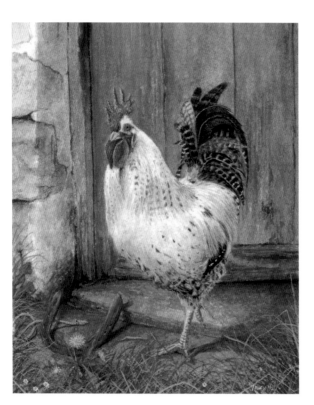

SCUMBLED WATERCOLOUR
Lucky Cockerel by Tracy Hall
For her painting, the artist has cleverly adapted the scumbling method to watercolour to build up the textures of the stonework and barn door. She has used the paint with the minimum of water and glazed over the scumbled areas when dry.

TIPS: TEXTURING

• A bristle brush is ideal for scumbling, but other possibilities include stencilling brushes, sponges, crumpled tissue paper or even your fingers. If you do use a softer brush, make sure it is an old one that can take some rough treatment – a good brush will soon be ruined.

• Practise your technique on some spare paper. Load the brush well with dry paint, then, with a twisting, dabbing motion of the brush head, 'grind' the paint into the paper. Repeat the process for a delightfully varied texture.

• Like other texture-creating techniques, scumbling works best in contrast with smoother, less textured area, so keep it localized to small areas of your painting – an all-over scumbled texture will lose impact.

APPLYING INITIAL COLOURS

1 The edge of the mountain is covered with masking fluid and left to dry. The paper is dampened, and a wash of Antwerp Blue with a touch of Payne's Gray is laid. The colour is lifted out where it floods over the mountain top.

SCUMBLING DRY COLOUR

2 The shadows on the mountain are painted with a darker, greyer mix of the two colours used previously. When the paint is dry, dry sepia is scumbled on the exposed rock edges and used to pepper snow in the centre.

3 A diluted but dry mixture of Antwerp Blue and Payne's Gray is used to scumble the trampled snow in the foreground. Tone is built up by further scumbling.

4 The masking fluid is carefully rubbed off and the white areas are dampened. A pale wash of Antwerp Blue is applied for the shadows in the undulating snow. The crispness of the edge of the snow-covered mountain provides a pleasing contrast to the scumbled marks in the foreground.

PLANNING THE LAYERS

Experiment with scumbling to see the effects you can get. Try applying light colours over dark, dark over light or a vivid colour over a contrasting one.

CREATING TEXTURE

THERE ARE TWO MAIN KINDS OF TEXTURE IN PAINTING: SURFACE TEXTURE, IN WHICH THE PAINT ITSELF IS BUILT UP OR MANIPULATED IN SOME WAY TO CREATE WHAT IS KNOWN AS SURFACE INTEREST; AND IMITATIVE TEXTURE, IN WHICH A CERTAIN TECHNIQUE IS EMPLOYED TO PROVIDE THE PICTORIAL EQUIVALENT OF A TEXTURE SEEN IN NATURE.

Surface texture is sometimes seen as an end in itself, but in many cases it is a welcome by-product of the attempt to turn the three-dimensional world into a convincing two-dimensional image. Since watercolours are applied in thin layers, they cannot be built up to form surface texture, but this can be provided instead by the grain of the paper. There are a great many watercolour papers on the market, some of which – particularly the handmade varieties – are so rough that they appear almost to be embossed. Rough papers can give exciting effects, because the paint will settle unevenly (and not always predictably), breaking up each area of colour and leaving flecks of white showing through.

Acrylic paints are ideal for creating surface interest because they can be used both thickly and thinly in the same painting,

providing a lively contrast. You can vary the brushmarks, using fine, delicate strokes in some places and large, sweeping ones in others.

Several of the best-known techniques for making paint resemble rocks, tree bark, fabrics and so on are described in other entries, but there are some other tricks of the trade. One of these – unconventional but effective – is to mix watercolour paint with soap. The soap thickens the paint without destroying its translucency. Soapy paint stays where you put it instead of flowing outwards, and allows you to use inventive brushwork to describe both textures and forms.

Intriguingly unpredictable effects can be obtained by a variation of the resist technique. If you lay down some turpentine or paint thinner on the paper and then paint over it, the paint and the oil will separate to give a marbled appearance.

SUGGESTED APPLICATIONS

• Study the texture you wish to evoke, then choose an applicator that will reproduce that texture.

APPLYING PAINT WITH PAPER
Venice by Moira Huntly
To suggest the beautiful crumbling plaster walls of the buildings, the artist brushed watercolour onto a thick piece of paper, then pressed it firmly onto the working surface. The effect of this technique will vary depending on the texture of the paper and the thickness of the paint.

> ### SEE ALSO
> Dry-brush, 68–69
> Wax resist, 80–81
> Sponging, 82–83
> Spattering, 84–85
> Scumbling, 92–93

INITIAL DRAWING AND PAINTING
1 First, the artist draws the basket in lightly, and then applies washes to the background, foreground and to the basket itself. The paint is left to dry completely.

BUILDING TEXTURE

2 Shadowed areas are painted in, and, while the paint is still wet, the textured side of a piece of paper towel is pressed into it to lift off some of the paint and leave an imprint of the paper behind. The paint is then left to dry.

3 Spots of darker colour are then dabbed onto the basket using bubble wrap, bubble-side out, to suggest the mottled, textured weave of the basket.

4 When this is dry, a strip of corrugated cardboard is used to apply paint for the woven border along the top edge of the basket.

5 An imaginative application of paint, using the kind of scrap materials that most people have in their homes, has resulted in the almost tactile surface texture of this basket.

ALUMINIUM FOIL AND CLINGFILM

Striking effects to create a range of features – twisting ridges and edges, a texture of sharp lines and dark-and-light patches – can be achieved with aluminium foil. Try this experiment. Have a crumpled sheet of aluminium foil at the ready. Apply three broad bands of colour wet-on-dry, allowing them to blend. Press the sheet of aluminium foil onto the paint. Press it gently all over so the crumpled surface is in contact with the still-damp watercolour. When the paint has dried, remove the foil, and see its texture imprinted onto the page. Try the same technique with clingfilm.

Applying the washes

Pressing on the foil

The final effect

BODY COLOUR

THIS SLIGHTLY CONFUSING TERM SIMPLY MEANS OPAQUE WATER-BASED PAINT. IT CAN BE USED TO GREAT EFFECT WITH THE MORE CONVENTIONAL TRANSLUCENT WATERCOLOUR.

SEE ALSO

Wet-in-wet, pages 44–45
Toned ground, pages 70–71
Reserving highlights, 74–75

In the past the term 'body colour' was generally used to describe Chinese White mixed with transparent watercolour and applied to parts of a painting, or the same white used straight from the tube for highlights. Today, however, it is often employed as an alternative term for opaque gouache paint.

Some watercolour painters avoid the use of body colour completely, priding themselves on achieving all the highlights in a painting by reserving areas of white paper. There are good reasons for this, because the lovely translucency of watercolour can be destroyed by the addition of body colour, but opaque watercolour is an attractive medium when used sensitively.

A watercolour that has gone wrong – perhaps become overworked or too bright in one area – can often be saved by overlaying a semi-opaque wash, and untidy highlights can be cleaned up and strengthened in the same way.

SUGGESTED APPLICATIONS

• Transparent watercolour mixed with either Chinese White or gouache Zinc (not Flake) White is particularly well suited to creating subtle weather effects in landscapes, such as mist-shrouded hills. The mixture gives a milky, translucent effect slightly different from that of gouache itself, which has a more chalky, pastel-like quality.

LAYING A TONED GROUND

1 First, a toned ground is laid down over the entire surface, using acrylic paint in a pale beige-cream. When this is dry, the buildings, trees and foreground are painted in with Ultramarine, Prussian Blue, Alizarin Crimson and Sap Green watercolour. Washes of these colours are painted wet-in-wet, using a large brush and loose brushstrokes. There is little form or definition at this stage of the painting.

BUILDING THE SKY AND FOREGROUND

2 When the washes are dry, body colour is used to build up the sky. The artist uses gouache in white, Lemon Yellow, Indian Yellow and a neutral grey.

3 White, Saffron Green and Indian Yellow gouache are applied to the grassy area in the foreground, deliberately echoing the colours of the sky. Patches of especially solid body colour here create the effect of dappled sunlight.

ADDING FINAL DETAILS

4 Further details, such as trunks and branches, are added to the trees, using Olive Green and Prussian Blue watercolour. The artist then dabs on touches of pale yellow gouache to highlight some of the leaves on the trees in the foreground.

5 The mixture of misty, blue-mauve watercolour and sharp, solid gouache creates a highly atmospheric scene, reminiscent of the colours on a sunny early morning.

BEING SELECTIVE

• Use body colour selectively – restricting it to parts of the painting so that it contrasts with the more translucent washes will have the greatest impact.

MIXED MEDIA

ALTHOUGH MANY ARTISTS KNOW THAT THEY CAN CREATE THEIR BEST EFFECTS WITH PURE WATERCOLOUR, MORE AND MORE ARE BREAKING AWAY FROM CONVENTION, FINDING THAT THEY CAN CREATE LIVELIER AND MORE EXPRESSIVE PAINTINGS BY COMBINING THE ATTRIBUTES OF SEVERAL DIFFERENT MEDIA.

To some extent, mixing media is a matter of trial and error, and there is now such a diversity of artists' materials that there is no way of prescribing techniques for each one or for each possible combination. However, it can be said that some mixtures are easier to manage than others. Acrylic and watercolour, for example, can be made to blend into one another almost imperceptibly because they have similar characteristics, but two or more physically dissimilar media, such as line and wash, will automatically set up a contrast. There is nothing wrong with this – it may even be the point of the exercise – but it can make it difficult to preserve an overall unity.The only way to explore the natures of the different materials and find out the most effective means of using them is to try out various combinations.

SUGGESTED APPLICATIONS
• Develop a sensitivity to your subject matter and choose media accordingly, to evoke a corresponding impression, mood and texture.

Water-based media
Acrylic used thinly, diluted with water but without the addition of white or any medium, behaves in more or less the same way as watercolour. There are two important differences between them, however. One is that acrylic has greater depth of colour so that a first wash can, if desired, be extremely vivid, and the other is that, once dry, the paint cannot be removed. This can be an advantage, as further washes, either in watercolour or acrylic, can be laid over an initial one without disturbing the pigment. The paint need not be applied in thin washes throughout: the combination of shimmering, translucent watercolour and thickly painted areas of acrylic can be very effective, particularly in landscapes with strong foreground interest, where you want to pick out small details like individual flowers or grass heads (very hard to do in watercolour).

Gouache and watercolour are often used together, and many artists scarcely differentiate between them. However, unless both are used thinly, it can be a more difficult combination to manage, since gouache paint, once mixed with white to make it opaque, has a matt surface, which can make it look dead and dull beside a watercolour wash.

Ink and watercolour are another successful combination, as demonstrated in the example on the facing page.

CAPTURING DETAIL
The Pink Umbrella by Paul Dawson
Every surface in this picture is treated with the same loving attention to detail to create its meticulously rendered realistic effects. These include dry-brush over preliminary wash to texture the floorboards, table and walls; the leaves were added with thick gouache on top. For the chair, a wash was laid, then the cane weave was defined with ink and finished with fine glazes of acrylic.

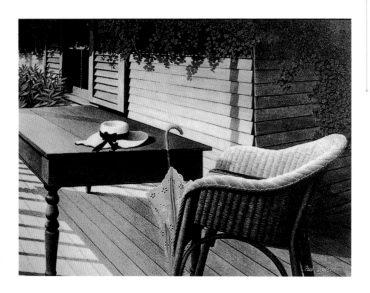

TIPS: 'RESCUING' WORK

• It is often possible to save an unsuccessful watercolour by turning to acrylic in the later stages.

• Try using a failed watercolour as a basis for experimentation; many successful mixed-media paintings are less the result of advance planning than of exploratory reworking.

BUILDING UP WITH DIFFERENT MEDIA

2 She continues to build up the tones, using a mixture of ink and gum arabic.

LAYING A TONED GROUND

1 To create a toned ground that will unite the whole image, cyan acrylic ink is first dripped onto damp paper and spread and rubbed in with paper towel. Using an ink dropper, the artist then draws in some rough outlines with coloured ink. While the ink is still wet, she blocks in areas of darker tone with a paintbrush and ink mixed with gum arabic.

3 She paints the sunflower petals in yellow gouache, an opaque colour.

4 The finished picture shows how well the two media complement each other. The patchy, translucent, blue-green ink washes provide the perfect contrast to the strong, flat, yellow gouache of the flower petals.

Watercolour and pastel

Soft pastels can be used very successfully with watercolour and provide an excellent means of adding texture and surface interest to a painting.

Overlaying a watercolour wash with light strokes of pastel, particularly on a fairly rough paper, can create sparkling broken colours.

Oil pastels have a slightly different, but equally interesting effect. A light layer of oil pastel laid down under a watercolour wash will repel the water to a greater or lesser degree (some oil pastels are oilier than others) so that it sinks only into the troughs of the paper, resulting in a slightly mottled, granular area of colour.

Gouache and pastel

These two media have been used together since the eighteenth century when pastel was at the height of its popularity as an artist's medium. Some mixed-media techniques are based on the dissimilarity of the elements used, which creates its own kind of tension and dynamism; however, gouache and pastel are natural partners, having a similar matt, chalky quality.

Watercolour crayons

These are, in effect, mixed media in themselves. When dry, they are a drawing medium, but as soon as water is applied to them, they liquefy to become paint that can be spread with a brush. Highly varied effects can be created by using them in a linear manner in some parts of a painting and as paints in others. They can also be combined with traditional watercolours, felt-tipped pens or pen and ink.

SEE ALSO
....
Line and wash, pages 72–73
Wax resist, pages 80–81

WATERCOLOUR AND COLLAGE
Polish Rooster by Carolyn Wilson
This painting began with a watercolour underpainting on thick paper, which was then collaged with various textured oriental rice papers, using acrylic matt medium as the glue. The collaged pieces were torn, not cut. When the paper was dry, a further layer of colour was added.

TOUCHES OF GOLD
Apples in a Papier Maché Bowl
by Clare Brooks
At first sight, this painting appears
to be simply a watercolour, but the
artist has been highly innovative and
inventive, using gold powder added to
aqua pasta for the patterns around the
edges of the bowl, and employing the
sgraffito technique for the markings
inside the bowl. By mixing the colours
for the apples with gum arabic, she
was able to slow the drying time and
thus make the paint more workable.

OTHER MEDIA

The only limit to mixed-
media work is your
imagination and skill, so
experiment with as many
different combinations as
you like. Try watercolour
with charcoal and pencil,
or with conté crayon or
coloured wax crayon.

CORRECTING MISTAKES

IT IS A COMMON BELIEF THAT WATERCOLOURS CANNOT BE CORRECTED BUT, IN FACT, THERE ARE SEVERAL WAYS OF MAKING CHANGES, CORRECTING OR MODIFYING PARTS OF A PAINTING.

Before painting complete pictures, you'll need to know how to correct mistakes. Every watercolourist may sometimes find that a wash has gone over an edge that was meant to be clean, or decide halfway through a picture that a colour isn't quite right. It is comforting to know that there are remedies.

The methods depend on how far you have progressed with your painting. Paint can be removed by lifting out with a sponge and clean water, but you can lift paint out more radically by actually washing it off. If you notice at an early stage that something is badly awry – perhaps the proportions are wrong or an initial colour doesn't look right – put the entire painting under cold running water and gently sponge off the paint.

In the later stages of a picture, you may want to change a small area without disturbing the surrounding colours. In this case, dab off the paint with a dampened sponge, and let the paper dry before repainting. For tiny areas, you can use a dampened cotton bud or wet brush, which is also ideal if you want to add highlights or soften over-hard edges.

Sometimes you may find that a white area has been spoiled by small flecks and spatters of paint. You can touch these out with opaque white, but a better method is to remove them by scraping with the flat edge of a cutting or craft knife; don't use the point which could dig into the paper and spoil the surface.

CORRECTING THE SPREAD OF COLOUR
If one colour floods into another to create an unwanted effect, the excess can be mopped up with a small sponge or piece of blotting paper.

UNEXPECTED EFFECTS

Don't be in too much of a hurry to correct a 'mistake'. One of the charms of watercolour is its ability to produce unexpected effects. Allow yourself to be led by the medium to a certain extent, and see if you can work with those 'happy accidents', making them look like an intentional part of the finished piece.

SCRAPING AWAY BLEMISHES
Small specks and spatters are easily removed by scraping with a knife or razor blade. This must be done with care, however, or the blade might tear holes in the paper.

SPONGING OFF EXCESS COLOUR
If there is too much colour in one area, some can be lifted out with a damp sponge.

CLEANING UP EDGES
Ragged edges can either be tidied up with a knife, as in the top example, or with opaque white gouache paint, as here.

SOFTENING A SHADOW

1 A shadow in the foreground is too hard-edged. The artist washes away part of it with a sponge dipped in clean water.

2 The edges of the shadow are successfully softened but the divisions between the light and dark areas are now insufficiently defined. The aim is to give a crisp, dappled effect, similar to the shadow below the fountain.

3 A little more of the mauve-blue watercolour is applied at the back of the shadow and left to dry. Then a mixture of red watercolour and white gouache, carefully matched to the pinks of the courtyard paving, is painted over the blue shadow.

CORRECTING A PAINT RUN

1 The artist is painting a background to a family portrait when the wash that he is applying bleeds onto one of the foreground figures.

2 If you experience accidental spills, use a tissue quickly to mop up any of the accidental colour.

3 It is easy to correct mistakes as you go along. Here some hair colour was spilt onto the cheek and was lifted off with a damp flat brush.

SEE ALSO

Lifting out, pages 56–57
Reserving highlights, pages 74–75
Scraping back, pages 76–77

PICTURE-MAKING

Whatever the medium used, there are certain principles an artist needs to know, such as understanding tonal values and the optical illusions of perspective and three-dimensional form. Developing a personal language, maintaining the practice of sketching and knowing how to make a good composition are universal, too.

But certain factors are more relevant just to watercolour. For example, the translucency of the medium means that you can't simply paint over a mistake, as you can in, say, oils, so planning your work ahead is essential. Similarly, a wash of one colour laid over another will alter the colour of both, so a knowledge of the way in which colours interact is especially important for the watercolourist. This section explains all the basic principles that allow the artist to translate three-dimensional reality onto the two-dimensional plane.

THE PRIMARY PALETTE

THE PRIMARY COLOURS ARE THE THREE FUNDAMENTAL COLOURS WHICH ARE MIXED TO CREATE ALL OTHER COLOURS IN THE PAINTER'S PALETTE. THERE ARE TWO SETS OF PRIMARIES: ADDITIVE AND SUBTRACTIVE.

THE COLOUR WHEEL

This colour wheel attempts to accommodate both systems. It uses Quinacridone Magenta, Aureolin Yellow and Cobalt Blue as primary colours. Admittedly the Cobalt Blue is not a true cyan, but neither is Cerulean, Phthalo, Manganese or Ultramarine. Cobalt Blue mixes well with other pigments, which some would say partially makes up for its limitations.

Perhaps you remember learning at school about the three 'primary' colours – red, yellow and blue – from which all other colours can be mixed. But just which particular red, which yellow and which blue does this refer to? To complicate matters further, there is more than one kind of primary colour. There are the light or 'additive' colour primaries, that you see through light, as in a television or on a computer screen; and pigment or 'subtractive' colour primaries, that you see as paint pigments or inks. Artists need to consider both types when painting. Colours are mixed according to the subtractive pigment primaries, and then our eyes evaluate the colours we use through the additive light primaries.

PRIMARIES MIX TO GREY

The three pigment primaries mixed together make grey.

LIGHT OR ADDITIVE COLOUR PRIMARIES
When we mix colours of light, the more we mix the brighter the colour gets. Colours add to each other. By mixing just three colours of light – red, green and blue – we can make any colour we want. These are the primary colours used to make the millions of different colours we see on television and computer screens.

PIGMENT OR SUBTRACTIVE COLOUR PRIMARIES
Paints and pigments absorb different colours of light, subtracting from what you see. The more pigment is added, the more light is absorbed and the darker the combined colour becomes. It is nearly the opposite of mixing light. The primary colours for paint or pigments are cyan, magenta and yellow (these, along with black, are the four colours used in colour printing and to create the printed colours you see on this page). Mixing the three pigment primaries produces black or grey, as well as all other pigment colours.

PRIMARIES MIX TO SECONDARIES
Two pigment primaries mix together to make a secondary colour. Primaries with secondaries provide a full range of colours.

1 Yellow
Aureolin Yellow

2 Yellow-orange
New Gamboge

3 Red-orange
Cadmium Orange

4 Red
Cadmium Red

5 Magenta
Quinacridone Magenta

6 Red-violet
Quinacridone Violet

7 Blue-violet
Carbazole Violet (Dioxazine)

8 Middle blue
French Ultramarine

9 Cyan
Cobalt Blue

10 Turquoise
Cerulean Blue

11 Green-blue
Ultramarine Turquoise

12 Yellow-green
Green Gold

Magenta + yellow = orange   Yellow + cyan = green   Magenta + cyan = blue-violet

Choosing primary palettes

Because the pigment primaries mix to create all other colours, an artist can use just three pigments for a painting. These three studies of the same subject use only primary colours of different kinds of watercolour pigment. Why not try it out yourself: choose three primaries that have the characteristics you want – and go!

PERMANENT, STAINING PIGMENTS

John Deyloff selected three permanent, staining primaries for his study: Phthalo Blue, Holbein's Opera and Quinacridone Gold. Note the very dark darks that he was able to mix from these three pigments – as well as some lighter greys. Transparent washes are more difficult to obtain with these strong pigments.

TRANSPARENT, NON-STAINING PIGMENTS

Jan Hart played with three of her favourite pigments, which demonstrate a bit of granulation (in the Cobalt Blue), transparency and nice variation in colours. Note that achieving very dark darks is not as easy with this palette of primaries. The colours chosen were: Cobalt Blue, Rose Madder Genuine and Aureolin Yellow

SEDIMENTARY OR OPAQUE PIGMENTS

Karen Norris chose three sedimentary or opaque pigments for her study. Her selection enabled her to create some interesting textures and pigment mixtures, as well as some sense of transparency. Quinacridone Burnt Scarlet is not a sedimentary pigment, but the artist chose to include it with the two that are – Ultramarine Blue and New Gamboge.

Phthalo Blue	Cobalt Blue	Quinacridone Burnt Scarlet
Opera (Holbein)	Rose Madder Genuine	Ultramarine Blue
Quinacridone Gold	Aureolin Yellow	New Gamboge

COMPLEMENTARY AND ANALOGOUS PALETTES

IT IS SAID THAT NO COLOUR IS MORE BEAUTIFUL, MORE EXCITING OR MORE VIBRANT THAN WHEN IT IS PLACED NEXT TO ITS COMPLEMENT – ITS PARTNER – ACROSS THE COLOUR WHEEL.

On the colour wheel, the complement of a primary colour (magenta, cyan or yellow) is the combination of the other two primaries. So mixing a colour and its complement is the same as mixing all three primaries together. The complementary palette is a simple, easy-to-use colour scheme with potential for the strongest colour contrasts.

The analogous palette offers the artist adjacent, closely related pigments that combine in perfect harmony. Each pigment contains a part of its neighbour, which makes them all related. Many people who grew up in the 'dyed to match' culture of the 1950s, when orange and red were thought to clash, only learned years later to appreciate the rich harmony of the analogous hues. Choose a minimum of three adjacent colours to explore the interesting ways in which this palette can be used to promote the desired feeling and mood.

The studies of a pink rose (opposite) demonstrate the effects that the analogous palette can produce. The close relationship between the colours results in great coherence in the finished painting. Some artists enjoy combining high-chroma (pure and vivid) pigments with low-chroma, more 'muddy' ones within an analogous scheme.

TIPS: CHOOSING COMPLEMENTARY SCHEMES

• For a complementary scheme, think 'contrast'.

• In a complementary scheme, the most striking colour choice is a warm and a cool. 'Warm' colours are reds, oranges and similar pigments; 'cool' colours are blues and greens.

• Consider using a warm, pure colour (red or orange) as an accent placed opposite unsaturated cool colours to emphasize the warms – or vice versa.

• For best results choose a dominant complementary that will appear directly and in mixes. Use the other complementary for accents.

• Avoid overuse of unsaturated warm colours such as brown or dull yellow. Overuse tends to create a deadening effect.

THE COMPLEMENTARY COLOUR WHEEL
Yellow's complement, blue-violet, is a mix of magenta and cyan. Blue-violet plus yellow = dark grey or black.

Yellow

Magenta

Cyan

Blue-violet

USING A COMPLEMENTARY PALETTE
Beyond the Coyote Fence by Allen Brown
Allen Brown selected Cadmium Orange and Ultramarine Blue as complementary colours for his painting. His colour choices appear to be consistent with the pigment colour wheel. Although he used pure Cadmium Orange very sparingly and pure Ultramarine Blue even more sparingly, his deft use of both for mixing colourful neutrals is quite apparent. He made a conscious choice to use more Ultramarine Blue than Cadmium Orange to give the cool bias his winter landscape needed.

Cadmium Orange

Ultramarine Blue

ANALOGOUS COLOUR WHEELS

The first pigment wheel (right) shows close analogous colour relationships, and the second pigment wheel (far right) shows one step or looser relationships. Try both and see the different possibilities.

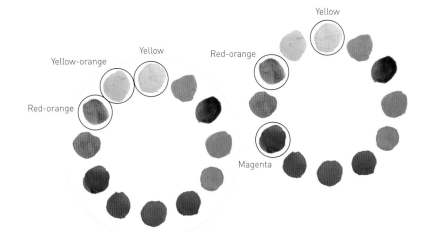

Red-orange
Yellow-orange
Yellow
Red-orange
Yellow
Red-orange
Yellow
Magenta

TIPS: CHOOSING ANALOGOUS SCHEMES

• For an analogous colour scheme think 'co-ordination'; the analogous scheme is inherently harmonious.

• When using an analogous scheme, the choice of appropriate subject matter is all-important – it too needs to have harmony of colour. In the case of greens, the analogous colour scheme is fully visible in nature: Remember this in your next summer landscape.

PURE, HIGH-CHROMA PIGMENTS

The use of three or four adjacent high-chroma pigments on the visual colour wheel certainly grabs attention with its sizzle. It can overwhelm the eye if the high-chroma pigments are used purely and at full strength. Even mixes of these intense pigments create a vibrant painting. Here the Quinacridone Magenta provides some relief in the background. Rose Madder Genuine was used as an underwash.

LOW-CHROMA, SEMI-NEUTRAL

Each of these pigments is located away from the high chroma rim of the pigment map. Together they comprise 'neutralized' violet, red and red-orange, along with some wonderful granulations. A distinctive mood of mystery, or cloaked danger, is evoked by these semi-neutrals. Note the rich creeping and granulating in the mixes. An underwash of pale English Red Earth helped to set the sombre mood.

HIGH- AND LOW-CHROMA

You can combine two high-chroma pigments and one low-chroma, or two low and one high, as shown. A simple, elegant colour scheme can consist of three carefully selected analogous paints – two of low chroma and a single high-intensity pigment. Here the dusky Purpurite Genuine and smooth Venetian Red were selected as the red-violet and red-orange, respectively. The central magenta position was claimed by the vibrant Opera – a 'hot pink' that is really cool in temperature.

| Vermillion | Opera (Holbein) | Quinacridone Magenta | Rose Madder Genuine | Venetian Red | Purpurite Genuine | Napthamide Maroon | English Red Earth | Venetian Red | Opera (Holbein) | Purpurite Genuine |

CHOOSING A PALETTE

WHEN STARTING A WATERCOLOUR, IT CAN BE TEMPTING SIMPLY TO 'PAINT WHAT YOU SEE' – THAT IS, TO USE THE WHOLE RANGE OF COLOURS THAT YOU PERCEIVE IN THE SUBJECT IN FRONT OF YOU. BUT FOR A MORE EFFECTIVE RESULT, IT IS BETTER TO WORK WITH A UNIQUE COLOUR PALETTE.

When choosing a colour palette to work with, be aware that the more colours you use in a painting, the more difficult it is to achieve colour harmony. Restraint and a considered use of colour will result in a more harmonious finished piece that will be more pleasing to the eye, as well as conveying mood and a sense of artistic authority.

An artist's 'palette' – the colour scheme used in a painting – is a specific choice of colours based on their relationship to each other on the colour wheel. Many artists resist colour schemes – until they try one. Using a colour scheme is an effective way to extend your understanding of colours and colour relationships.

It's well worth investing some time experimenting with various palettes. As your understanding grows, you'll be better placed to choose the palette that is most sympathetic to your subject matter, and that will produce the effect you want. Your command of colour scheming will contribute significantly to the 'mood' of your painting and the blending of all the elements into a coherent whole. You may be surprised to discover the range of colours and tones you can achieve with just a limited number of pigments. The studies shown here all feature the same subject yet, because the same palette isn't used in each case, the final results look and feel different. As well as these options, there are others to explore.

TIPS: CHOOSING COLOURS

• For best results in an analogous scheme, avoid combining warm and cool colours.

• Use the monochromatic Velásquez, and complementary palettes (see pages 112–113) to learn about value/tone relationships and/or as value studies for another painting.

• To maintain control and restraint in your use of colours, try putting tape over the paints in your palette that you intend not to use.

MONOCHROMATIC PALETTE

Using a single colour in variations of lightness and saturation makes for easy viewing and can establish an overall mood. It also forces the artist to think in terms of tonal values (see pages 116–117). Here Manganese Violet, representing the red-violet in the colour wheel, was selected as much for its texture as for its colour. Note how the granulation provides additional interest. However, in a monochromatic scheme it can be difficult to distinguish the most important element of the painting since all parts are rendered in different tonal values of a single colour.

Red-violet

Manganese Violet

ANALOGOUS PALETTE

This colour scheme (see page 109) offers the strongest potential for creating unity and a particular mood. It is as easy to use as the monochromatic scheme, but it looks richer. Using paint colours that are immediately adjacent to one another creates a singular boldness – there is no colour contrast. A painting done in an analogous scheme can encompass all cool colours for a sombre or night-time scene, or all warm colours for a lighter portrayal.

It is possible to select immediately adjacent hues for a 'tight' study, or hues that are separated by one colour step for a 'loose' study. It also is possible to select analogous pigments that are located in more neutral positions on the colour wheel, such as greens or red-violets, for more neutral mood possibilities. Above all, this colour scheme encourages you to step out of your comfort zone.

Carbazole Violet (Dioxazine)   Quinacridone Magenta   Quinacridone Burnt Orange

Tight palette

Red
Magenta
Red-violet

Loose palette

Red-orange
Magenta
Blue-violet

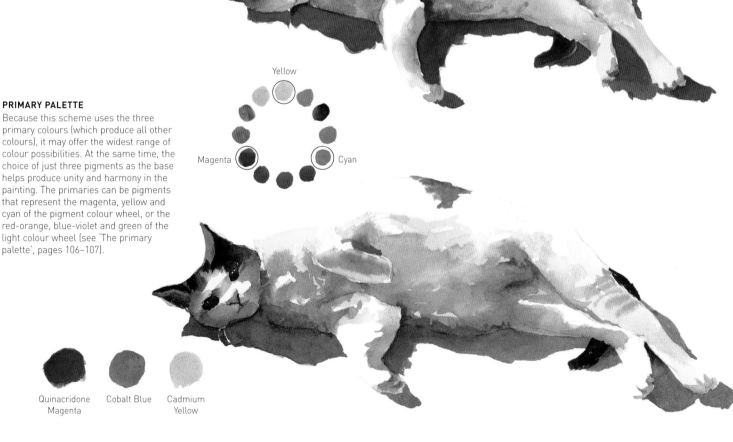

PRIMARY PALETTE

Because this scheme uses the three primary colours (which produce all other colours), it may offer the widest range of colour possibilities. At the same time, the choice of just three pigments as the base helps produce unity and harmony in the painting. The primaries can be pigments that represent the magenta, yellow and cyan of the pigment colour wheel, or the red-orange, blue-violet and green of the light colour wheel (see 'The primary palette', pages 106–107).

Yellow
Magenta
Cyan

Quinacridone Magenta   Cobalt Blue   Cadmium Yellow

THE VELÁSQUEZ PALETTE

Named for Spanish artist Diego Velásquez, this is a subtle version of the primary pigment palette, using a limited selection of three to four pigments that were available to the old oil-painting masters. The Yellow Ochre, Burnt Sienna and Ultramarine Blue combine to create soft neutrals and glowing lights, as shown in the study. Modernize the palette by substituting Quinacridone Gold for Yellow Ochre and Quinacridone Burnt Orange for Burnt Sienna. Ultramarine Blue remains a long-time favourite of many artists and a staple of their palettes. You can achieve a wonderful glow with these pigments. The pale green is achieved by mixing Yellow Ochre and Ultramarine. Although Ultramarine and Burnt Sienna cannot create lavender, the neutral achieved is most useful.

Yellow Ochre   Ultramarine   Burnt Sienna
                Blue

PAINT A COLOUR WHEEL

You can build your own colour wheel and take it with you when you paint. It is a good idea to keep any colour wheels that you create very simple. There should be a lot of room for individual interpretation and substitution of pigments when something new and exciting comes out. When a new pigment comes out, add it to your existing colour wheel to fill in the gaps or do a new colour wheel – just to find out what your current thinking is.

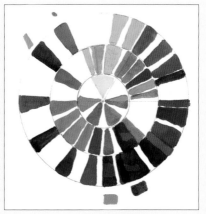

COMPLEMENTARY PALETTE

Using pure colour opposites (see 'The Colour Wheel', page 106) enables you to present a stronger contrast than in any other colour scheme, thus drawing maximum attention. For the best results, place cool colours against warm ones, or vice versa. The predominance in the amount of one colour over the other creates the intended mood. A night painting, for example, may start as a complementary colour scheme. Note the strong contrasts in this cat study.

Carbazole Violet (Dioxazine)

Aureolin Yellow

Yellow

Blue-violet

TIPS: GETTING THE MOST OUT OF A PALETTE

• Increase the richness of the complementary palette by using four colours in two complementary pairs, for example a blue-violet and a cyan complementing a yellow and a red-orange (see left).

• Try the 'split-complementary' scheme that places a single warm colour – say, a yellow – against three oppositional colours, such as a warm blue, a blue-violet and a violet (see below left).

• Use a six-colour scheme, consisting of three sets of complements: a magenta and a green; a yellow and a blue-violet; a blue and an orange. These three sets will allow you to mix a range of neutrals, from brown to grey, and each can be 'pushed' towards the pure colour for accents.

• Try a tertiary palette, using 'tertiary' colours that are defined as those mixed from one primary and one secondary, for example, red and green, or blue and orange. The tertiary palette is useful for achieving complementary neutrals, with accents. A predominantly warm or cool bias works best with this scheme.

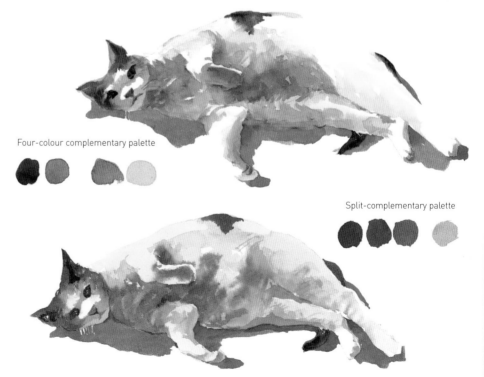

Four-colour complementary palette

Split-complementary palette

COLOUR MIXING AND OVERLAYING

WHEN MIXING COLOURS, REMEMBER THAT THEY ALWAYS LOOK DARKER WET, IN THE PALETTE, THAN THEY WILL DO ON THE PAPER.

TIPS

• Keep the water in your jar clean: dirty water may taint your colours. Refresh it often or use two jars – one of clean water for diluting paints, one for rinsing brushes.

• As you progress with the colour mixing, don't rely on the look of the colour on the palette – test it out on a spare piece of watercolour paper.

• Avoid mixing four or more colours together, or all you'll achieve is a characterless mud.

As explained on pages 106–107, the pigment primaries – red, yellow and blue – cannot be mixed from other colours. The secondaries, made from two primaries, and the tertiaries, made from the three primaries or one primary and a secondary, are also all available ready-made. However, you can achieve more variety through mixing – and it's fun. When you experiment with colour mixing, you will discover how dramatically the proportions of the pigments used affect the mixture and how much stronger some pigments are than others. The amount of water you add will affect the intensity of colour too.

If you don't achieve the colour you want when mixing wet, you can always adjust it by overlaying, in other words, 'mixing' colours on the paper rather than in the palette. This is comforting because it takes away the fear that nothing can be changed once it's down on paper. Don't rely too much on overpainting though; it's still best to achieve the right colour first time.

When mixing colours, don't always go for the obvious mix of pigments – or even the obvious tube or pan colour. You can get richer and subtler effects by combining more unlikely pigments.

RICH DARKS
There are many ways of achieving a dark mix other than using black directly from the pan or tube. One way is to mix Ultramarine Blue and Light Red. This combination makes a beautiful grey, with a large range of subtle hues that can be mixed in any strength up to a virtual black. Ultramarine Blue and Indian Red produce a more intense dark. Here Ultramarine Blue and Light Red are mixed on the palette to create a dark grey.

THE RIGHT GREEN
Manufacturers' greens are often very strong, and often too crude for the greens you see in nature. Rather than using a green straight from the tube or pan, start with a yellow such as Cadmium Lemon or New Gamboge. Add a smaller amount of a green, such as Phthalo Green or Hooker's Green, until the paint is the desired colour. Here Cobalt Teal was added to Permanent Yellow to get a bright green. Finally, add Burnt Umber or Burnt Sienna to the colour to tone it down and make it look more natural.

Overlaying colours

Because watercolours are transparent, you can't make a colour lighter by putting another one on top; you can only make it darker. And because of this transparency, you can't achieve a really dark colour with a first wash, as the white paper always shows through to some extent. It is done by laying one colour over another. You can also change colours by overlaying one on top of another; however, aim for no more than four layers of colour, as too many will spoil the fresh sparkle that is one of the most attractive features of watercolour.

WET VERSUS DRY

One of the trickiest aspects of watercolour painting is judging what the colour will look like when it's dry, so it's a good idea to do a test on a spare scrap of watercolour paper first. There can be considerable difference between a dry colour (top) and a wet one (bottom).

Raw Umber

French Ultramarine

French Ultramarine

Cadmium Yellow

Payne's Gray

Yellow Ochre

French Ultramarine

Alizarin Crimson

Cadmium Yellow

French Ultramarine

OVERLAYING TO DARKEN COLOUR

Some pigments are more transparent than others; to achieve the desired density, it may be necessary to overlay further layers of the same colour. The first layer should be completely dry and it is necessary to work quickly so that each new layer does not stir up the one beneath.

OVERLAYING TO LIGHTEN COLOUR

A light colour applied over a dark one does not disappear. Although you can change the nature of an underlying colour in this way, you can't significantly change its tonal value (see pages 116–117) unless you paint over it with a more opaque pigment.

OVERLAYING TO CHANGE COLOUR

Although you can alter a colour by laying another on top, you can't obliterate the first one – the new colour will be a mixture of the two.

TIPS: MIXING COLOURS

• Although you can add white to a watercolour mix to lighten it, you will alter its character totally, making it creamy and opaque. It is usually better to get paler tones by adding water rather than white paint.

• When painting a small area, use a small brush to add water to the colour on your mixing palette; a large brush would absorb too much colour and none would be left on the palette. Apply the colour to the paper with the same brush.

• When painting a large area, mix the water with the paint to form a reservoir on the palette, ensuring that sufficient paint is produced at the start to complete the wash without having to go back and mix more colour.

ANALYSING TONE

TONE, OR COLOUR VALUE, INDICATES THE DARKNESS OR LIGHTNESS OF A SUBJECT. EVERY COLOUR, AND WATERCOLOUR PAINT COLOUR, HAS ITS OWN VALUE.

All living beings use sight in practical ways; it is part of their 'survival kit'. Humans, for example, may use their sight to judge the distance between them and an oncoming car. However, humans' aesthetic use of sight is less well developed. An artist needs to cultivate this use of sight to look for relationships in the visual world – in colours, in shapes and in tones.

Tones – or 'tonal values' – refer to the relative lights and darks that we perceive in everything we see. Even in the absence of line and colour, we still know what we are looking at simply from the way in which these tones interrelate. The relative pattern of lights and darks in a drawing or painting helps to convey form and give an illusion of spatial depth, as well as contributing to its success as a composition. So it's not enough to know about colour; you need to have a good awareness of tone too.

TRANSLATING TONE TO COLOUR

Think of a black-and-white photograph. It contains no colour or lines, yet we can still 'read' the image perfectly well simply from the pattern of lights and darks and all the stages in-between. Doing studies like this one are a really good exercise and will heighten your awareness of tone.

BLACK-AND-WHITE PHOTOGRAPH

1 The children in this photograph, together with their reflections, make strong vertical shapes. Crossing the picture, there are the horizontal shapes of the bank and the ripples in the water. The absence of colour makes it easier to see this pattern.

TONAL SKETCH

2 In a linear drawing, edges are defined by lines – a pattern of lines is produced on the paper. In a tonal painting, edges are defined by areas of tone. The tonal pattern may overlap what would have been the line pattern; note how the children and their reflections make one continuous shape.

COLOUR SKETCH

3 In a coloured version of the same scene, the tones of the colours match those in the black-and-white tonal sketch.

IDENTIFYING TONAL CONTRASTS

When you are sketching outside, look for tonal contrasts. Which direction is the light coming from? On a sunny day this is easy to ascertain because shadows will be pronounced. Even though your logical mind may find it hard to believe, on a very bright day an intensely blue sky may actually be tonally darker than the buildings it illuminates. Conversely, on a dull day the land may be darker than the sea and sky.

SCOTTISH SEA SCENE

1 In this photograph of a Scottish scene on a damp, grey day the tonal contrast is between the sea, which reflects the sky, and the land.

2 In the resulting monochrome sketch (in which a yacht has been substituted for the boat), the land is much darker than the sky and water.

MEDITERRANEAN TONAL SKETCH

1 In this monochrome sketch, a white building is set against a searingly blue sky. In relation to the sky, the building appears much lighter and this is reflected in the greys used. Even without the addition of colour, the drawing conveys a powerful illusion of bright sunlight.

2 In this coloured version, the sky has been painted a deep blue to emphasize the contrast in tone between sky and building and to convey the warm, sunny light that is so reminiscent of the Mediterranean.

MAKE A TONAL PANEL

To help you understand tone, make some tonal panels. First make a panel with black and white paint. Then make others with neutral mixes, in various intensities.

BENCHMARK STRIP

1 Mark out a strip of 10 squares on a sheet of paper, making the size of the squares about 2cm (¾in). Now fill in the squares with paint, grading them from white to black (Chinese White and Ivory Black are good for this – usually, of course, it's not necessary to use black or white paint in watercolour. Start with white in the first square and add a minimal amount of black to increase the darkness of each subsequent square until reaching pure black. This tonal panel will act as a 'benchmark strip' for the tones in your painting.

COLOUR STRIP

2 Make a colour strip to compare with the benchmark strip. Start with a yellow. See how close in tone it is to the white compared to the blue, which is tonally much darker.

NEUTRAL STRIP

3 Make a third strip of squares. Mix a neutral grey from three primary colours, such as Cobalt Blue, Scarlet Lake and Aureolin Yellow. Use this mixture to make a panel that matches the benchmark strip in tonal value. Start with pure water in the first square to match the white paint, then use less water and more paint in the following squares. You will not achieve black, but you will be able to make a good dark tone. Now try the same procedure with others mixes of primary colours.

USING A TONAL PANEL

To practise recognizing tonal values, make a simple graded tonal panel of five 3.75cm (1½in) squares. Leave the first square blank to match your paper. Grade the tones in even steps towards a dark that is not quite black. Move this panel around your painting. Notice how the edge of the different squares in your strip will almost 'disappear' when matched with a part of your picture that is of the same tonal value.

CONTRASTING TONAL VALUES

1 In this bright, sunny painting, the tonal contrasts are very marked. The building – which is backlit by the sun and silhouetted – is a dark tone. The surrounding sky is much lighter.

SOFT TONAL VALUES

2 Playing down the tonal values between the reeds and the water – and emphasizing the contrast between the water lily and the water – focuses attention on the flower.

CLOSE TONAL VALUES

3 The leaves and fungi on this shady woodland floor are all very close in tone. There is just enough contrast to define the shapes.

USING A TONAL VIEWER

Colour can confuse your perception of values. An intense colour can appear lighter in value than it really is. A red, transparent Plexiglas square can help here. You may be able to order a piece cut to 7.5 x 7.5cm (3 x 3in) through your local glass shop. Or you can attach a small piece of red plastic to a blank slide mount. When you look through the red plastic, all the colours will be visible as values of light red to dark red.

LIGHT AGAINST DARK

Charisma by Jeanne Lamar
In this painting, the pale flowers stand out against the dark background, but even here there is considerable variety of tone, suggesting leaves and stems without being too specific.

LIGHT AND SHADOW

PAINTING IS ALL ABOUT LIGHT OR THE ABSENCE OF LIGHT. THROUGH LIGHT AND SHADOW WE UNDERSTAND FORM, TEXTURE AND COLOUR.

TIPS: A CAST SHADOW...

• ...is darkest, sharpest and coolest at its origin. It is always attached to the object that is casting it unless that object is in the air.

• ...is always transparent, allowing the underlying subject to show through.

• ...of a near or hard-edged object has hard edges. Shadows of distant or fuzzy objects have soft edges.

• ...changes as it passes over different surfaces. It may change in colour, direction and shape. For example, when the cast shadow of a roof overhang passes over a recessed area, such as a doorway or window frame, the shadow changes, usually dipping downwards.

• ...of a tree extending horizontally across the ground is linear and generally appears longer than it is wide. If you paint it very wide, it won't appear to lie flat on the ground. Shadows closest to the viewer are widest, warmest and darkest. Those further away become progressively thinner and cooler.

• ...of foliage often produces 'sun pictures' on the ground. The sun filters through the numerous openings of foliage to create irregular patterns of light. This is what we call 'dappled light'.

• ...may have colours of adjacent objects and even light reflected from another surface within it.

Manipulation of the lighting in a painting affects mood, so it is no wonder this aspect is one of the most essential in painting. One of the movements demonstrating this is Impressionism. The French Impressionists were known for capturing the transient effects of atmosphere and light, painting outdoors in the French countryside with its clear air and warm light. There they expressed what they saw – the incredible colours of light, shade and shadow. Creating shadow and light in watercolour is notoriously difficult but can be made easier by understanding the theory. Conversely, the beautiful translucency of the medium and its affinity with the glazing technique allows the artist to overlay areas of shadow that positively glow.

Colour in shadow

When asked the colour of shadows, most people reply, 'grey'. But shadows are never just grey. Conventional wisdom also suggests that the colour of shade (the part of the object turned away from the sun) is a darker shade of the object's local colour. However, colours from the surroundings are also reflected into the shadow, and the time of day plays a part too. Sunlight in early morning and late afternoon is warmer (more yellow) than direct light at noon, and so affects ambient colours and hence the colours reflected into the shadow.

CAST SHADOW
When a light source falls on an object, the cast shadow is the dark area that is caused by the object blocking the light source. The base colour of the cast shadow is the complement of the light source; here (above and right), the shadows are blue-violet with the complementary yellow-orange light source.

SHADE AND REFLECTED LIGHT
When a light ray bounces, its light waves become longer and the colour of the light becomes warmer. The shaded area receiving bounced light grows warm. This concept helps to explain why in bright sunlight we see orange in the shaded side of a building (left).

THE COLOUR OF SHADOWS

Under warm incandescent light, a tomato was placed on three different-coloured surfaces – pure white, dark green and yellow-gold. The direct yellow-orange light produces a blue cast shadow, which appears to our eyes as a combination of the shadow colour, surface colour and any reflected colour. The shadow's variable edge is due to other sources of light in the room.

TOMATO ON WHITE

On a pure white surface the cast shadow is blue. Within the cast shadow, closest to the base of the tomato, is some red reflected from the tomato creating an area of violet (red + blue). Note the band of reflected light from the white surface back onto the middle of the tomato.

TOMATO ON DARK GREEN

The colour of the cast shadow is still blue but it appears darker on the dark green surface colour. As the surface colour is reflected back onto the tomato, the combination is a dark neutral (red + green).

TOMATO ON YELLOW-GOLD

The cast shadow is the same blue – but now its visible colour is a mix of the blue and the yellow-gold surface – a pale greenish gold. Because the shadow is light enough, some of the reflected tomato red can be seen in the shadow. Yellow colour from the surface reflects back onto the tomato to create orange (red + yellow).

PAINTING CAST SHADOWS

These photographs and accompanying studies demonstrate choices in painting cast shadows.

POSTS AND MUD WALL

1 The sun shining from the upper left makes parallel beam shadows across the mud surface of the building in this photograph. When they reach the perpendicular light-coloured wall, the shadows change direction and colour. Note that the darkest, sharpest and coolest part of the shadow is at its origin – the base of the protruding beam.

SUNNY WALL

1 In the original photograph, the sun casts solid, hard-edged shadows of the rain spout and beam end (not shown) onto the sunny wall. Note the reflected light glow on the shaded left wall. A tree also casts its shadow onto the sunny wall in softened linear shapes and dappled sun pictures. The shadows change in colour as they fall over the white curtains.

2 An overall underwash of yellow anticipates the sunshine. The window is left as it is. Beginning with the shaded left wall, a bright mix of Rose Madder Genuine and yellow is brushed into the reflected light corner and pulled across to the left edge. While still wet, a darker mix of Rose Madder Genuine and Napthamide Maroon is blended in, leaving the upper corner alone. On the sunny wall, Rose Madder Genuine over the Aureolin Yellow is the perfect base for a darker and drier shadow mix applied with a round brush. Now the area is re-washed and more soft shadows added. Pure Cobalt Blue is applied to the window, using similar soft strokes for the cast shadow. Finally the harder-edged cast shadow from the left wall is added, using Cobalt Blue-Violet and taking care to paint the negative space around the sunlit grasses in the foreground.

2 The texture of the dried mud wall is achieved with granulating pigments, added directly into a still-wet base of Rose Madder Genuine. The undersides of the projecting beams are rendered warm and lighter, to suggest reflected light. The shadows are transparent Cobalt Blue, thinned and warmed up with Rose Madder Genuine as they move away from the beams.

WORKING WITH LIGHT SOURCES

WHATEVER THE SUBJECT YOU ARE PAINTING, THE PLACEMENT AND DIRECTION OF THE LIGHT SOURCE OR SOURCES WILL BE CRITICAL TO ITS SUCCESS. BE AWARE THAT SHADOWS CHANGE SHAPE AND DIRECTION THROUGH THE DAY – TAKE PHOTOS FOR REFERENCE AS YOU WORK.

As well as contributing to the overall mood of a painting, shadows serve various other important functions. For example, they act as an anchor, 'tying' an object to whatever surface it is standing on. If you're painting a pitcher on a table, for instance, and you leave out the shadow below it, the pitcher will look as if it's floating in space. They also help to create an illusion of three-dimensional space within the flat, two-dimensional surface of a painting, as well as introducing a sense of drama.

A shadow falls on the opposite side from which the light is coming – the object that casts it is blocking that light. You can vary the direction (and strength) of the shadow according to the effect you want to create, either by moving the object itself in relation to the light source or by altering the direction from which the light is coming. This is easiest if you are using artificial light – it could be as simple as moving the table lamp that is lighting your still life. If you are painting a portrait, you could ask the sitter to move so that the light, and therefore the shadow, falls differently on them.

To complicate matters a little, light often comes from more than one source, creating softer, secondary shadows in addition to the stronger main shadow. When observing your subject, be alert for such subtleties.

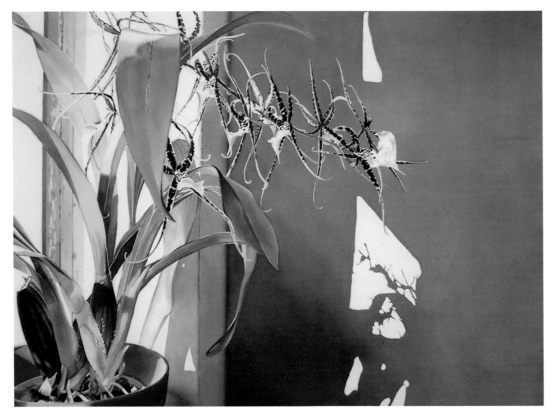

CREATING PATTERNS WITH LIGHT AND SHADOW

Frailty by Denny Bond
In this highly realistic painting, the artist has focused on the patches of light and the silhouette of the foliage cast on the wall to the right. Highlights on the foliage bring the plant forward in space, and the shadowed wall glows with reflected colour.

TIPS: CASTING SHADOWS

• The shape of a shadow is related to the shape of the object that casts it.

• Shadows are darkest close to the object.

• The darkness and definition of a shadow depends on how close it is to the light source. A strong, directional light will cast stronger, more clearly defined shadows than more diffused light.

HOW CAST SHADOWS WORK

In the original photograph, a strong, directional light is coming from the right of the vase, casting a strong shadow to the left. The lighting is simple and comes from a single source, so there are no secondary shadows. In the painting, the same colour is used for the cast shadow and the dark side of the vase. The yellowish cloth is painted around the shadow, overlapping it in the foreground just below the vase. Note how the shadow serves to 'anchor' the vase to the table – it is an essential part of the picture; without it the vase would float and there would be little sense of the space around it.

The colour of a shadow is affected by that of the surface on which it falls

The shape of the shadow is related to the shape of the object

Light from the side casts strong, clear shadows

Shadows are darkest close to the object

FLOWERPOTS ON A WINDOW LEDGE

Here, the strong directional light coming through the window casts diagonal shadows behind the flowerpots. In order to 'attach' the pots to the surface so that they don't appear to float, the artist has painted additional patches of shadow just behind the pots, right next to the base of each one. The strong shadows and highlights on petals, leaves and pots create a powerful sense of light flooding the whole scene.

THREE-DIMENSIONAL MODELLING

WHATEVER YOU ARE PAINTING, IN WHATEVER MEDIUM – WHETHER IT'S A TEACUP, A TREE OR A HUMAN FACE – THE WAY TO CREATE AN ILLUSION OF THREE-DIMENSIONAL SOLIDITY IS THROUGH THE USE OF LIGHT AND SHADE.

The form of any object is defined by the light that falls on it. The lightest and brightest parts are where the light strikes directly; the shaded or shadowed ones occur wherever the object blocking turns away from the light.

The intensity of the light and the texture of the object will determine the degree of contrast between light and dark areas, so you will first need to work out how dark the shadows are in relation to the highlights. This helps you decide how strong or weak each mixture should be.

When depicting the form of an object you should adapt your technique to suit its shape. Unless you are working wet-in-wet, watercolour washes naturally dry with hard edges. This is helpful when you're painting a building or table, where the divisions between the shaded and light-struck areas are clear. It is less so when you want to depict a rounded form with soft transitions between light and shade. Solve the problem by laying two or more washes side by side and blending them gently into one another.

OBJECTS WITH DEFINED EDGES

1 On square-edged objects like this, the divisions between light and shade are clear, and the shadowed side can be surprisingly dark.

BUILDING TONES

2 In the corresponding painting, a pale wash of pale yellow – the predominant colour – is first laid over nearly all of the object and background. Darker tones of the same colour are then applied to the surfaces away from the light – the inside of the box, the side closest to the viewer and the top edge of the back. The colour is applied wet-on-dry, to give crisp, defining edges. This instantly creates the illusion of three-dimensional solidity.

3 To make the box look even more convincing and to give surface interest, the grain of the wood is painted in with the tip of a small brush. However, the marks are still kept very light on the surfaces where the light strikes, so as not to destroy the convincing 3D effect.

CURVED OBJECTS

1 On curved surfaces like this flowerpot, the light areas flow into the darker ones with no obvious boundaries. In addition, in the case of surfaces that don't reflect much light such as terracotta, the contrast between light and shade, and the transition between them, may be quite subtle.

TIPS: LIGHT AND SHADOW

• Assessing lights and darks can be difficult because our eyes register colour first, rather than tone. A useful trick is to half-close your eyes, and to practise translating the objects you see into black and white photographs in your mind.

• When blending a dark area into a light one on a rounded object, take care not to overwork the paint. Too many blended overlays of colour can begin to look tired and muddy, so try to judge the strength of the darkest part correctly.

BLENDING WASHES

2 To paint the pot, the artist began by laying a light pink-brown wash and working darker colour into it while still wet. He created the mottled area with blobs of dark green dropped into very light yellow. Because the first washes were not allowed to dry, the dark colours blended softly into them.

3 The colours were strengthened all over the pot, and worked lightly into each other with a small paintbrush (above and right). The pot looks convincingly solid and rounded with the colour well blended but not overworked. The only hard edges visible are those on the rim of the pot and the tiny light strip on the left side.

PERSPECTIVE

THE PERCEIVED WORLD IS THREE-DIMENSIONAL, BUT THE PAINTER MUST TRANSLATE SPACE AND FORM IN A WAY THAT MAKES SENSE ON THE FLAT SURFACE OF A PIECE OF PAPER. ONE OF THE OPTICAL TRICKS THAT ARTISTS HAVE AT THEIR DISPOSAL IS LINEAR PERSPECTIVE.

Visual perception is the name for the way in which our brains interpret the messages from our eyes. One of the peculiarities of visual perception is that objects appear to get smaller the further away they are. Similarly, parallel lines, such as train tracks or furrows in a ploughed field, appear to converge in the distance, although of course in reality they maintain the same parallel relationship. This optical illusion is known as perspective (linear rather than aerial; see pages 128–129).

Discovered by Italian Renaissance artists, linear perspective became an obsession for some. Paulo Uccello, in particular, spent many hours experimenting with perspective and foreshortening (whereby the parts of an object appear to become compressed and smaller

the further away they are from the viewer). The results can be seen in his famous painting *The Battle of San Romano*, painted in the 1450s and now hanging in the National Gallery in London. The fallen lances on the ground all point towards a common vanishing point (the point at which parallel lines appear to converge) and the foreshortening of a fallen figure on the ground is thought to have been the first time that this technique was used.

Understanding and mastering perspective will allow you to create a sense of distance and scale in your images, to show objects overlapping, getting smaller or converging in an orderly and understandable way.

CONVERGING LAVENDER ROWS
1 This photo of a lavender field in the South of France clearly shows the effect of perspective, with the rows of lavender converging towards a vanishing point in the distance, leading the eye into the picture and towards the village in the background.

TIPS: PERSPECTIVE

• When working with perspective, remember that angles converge towards a common vanishing point, and that this vanishing point relates to the onlooker's viewpoint. In this painting of a lavender field, for example, we know without thinking that the onlooker is standing just left of the centre of the picture space, because the lavender rows here are hardly slanted at all but point straight ahead. Conversely, the rows on either side become progressively more angled the further they are from the onlooker.

• When assessing the perspective of an angular object such as a wall or building, hold a viewfinder or L-shaped frame up to it so you can accurately measure the angles against the right angles of the frame.

DOING A PERSPECTIVE DRAWING

2 The preliminary drawing shows the converging lines of the lavender rows. Some of the original details have been subtly altered for a more effective composition, and a few light initial washes have been laid.

BUILDING UP COLOUR AND DETAIL

3 Working from the back to the front, the artist begins adding colour and detail to the buildings in the village and the surrounding trees. The foreground lines are still visible.

4 The rows of lavender are loosely painted in with a violet, crimson and indigo mix, working wet-in-wet and sprinkling the wet paint with salt to create texture. Shadows are added to give a sense of form.

5 In the finished picture, colours and details have been strengthened. The rows of lavender clearly demonstrate the principles of perspective and show how useful this visual tool can be in creating the illusion of three-dimensional space on a flat, two-dimensional surface.

SPATIAL DEPTH

ONE OF THE CHALLENGES FACING THE ARTIST IS TO GIVE THE ILLUSION OF SPATIAL DEPTH, SOMETIMES KNOWN AS AERIAL PERSPECTIVE – IN OTHER WORDS, TO CONVEY THE SENSE THAT THERE IS A FOREGROUND, MIDDLE GROUND AND DISTANCE.

Using linear perspective (explained on pages 126–127) is one way of suggesting recession, but many subjects have few or no parallel lines, and this is where aerial perspective comes in. It's especially important for large, sweeping subjects such as landscapes.

Aerial perspective affects our visual perception in several ways. To begin with, the tiny particles of dust and moisture in the air affect the way we see colours, so that they become paler and paler towards the horizon, with the tonal contrasts minimal or imperceptible. Colours also become cooler, with a higher proportion of blue in them. A classic example is a landscape with hills, where the hills in the foreground are dark but become progressively paler in tone the further away they are. This effect can even be seen in photographs, recorded by the 'mechanical eye' of the camera lens.

In the same way as objects seem to become paler and 'cooler' the further away they are, they also become less defined, more hazy and less detailed. So, to create a sense of space, keep detail for foreground objects.

Tonal contrast is another way to increase the feeling of space. If all the colours in a picture are of a similar tone, the effect will be to flatten it. Sometimes, contrary to the principle that tones become paler with distance, darker tones in the background and paler ones in front can be effective. But this will depend on the subject matter and other factors need to be taken into account too, like the amount of definition and detail included with the paler foreground tones.

VENICE VIEW
In the painting shown being developed on the right and facing page, a deliberate decision was made not to paint in the sky and only to add a small amount of paint to the water, in order to maintain a sense of space. Cooler blues and browns – Cerulean Blue and Raw Sienna – are used for the lofty domes, and warmer ones – French Ultramarine and Burnt Sienna – for the bulk of the buildings and the foreground. This helps to achieve the huge spatial distances in the painting. Pure bright colours here and there, as on the striped parking poles, add vitality to the picture.

LAYING FOUNDATIONS
1 First, a broad pattern of light and dark is created, starting with a yellow wash overlaid with various strengths of violet. While the first yellow wash is still damp, quick, sure strokes of violet, applied with a small brush, are added to suggest the windows – this is all the detail they require as they are in the background. The tones behind the poles in the foreground are deepened to make them stand out, while the stripes on the poles in the middle distance differentiate them from their surroundings.

2 Tone and detail start to be added to give contrast and definition. The foreground posts are painted with a thin mix of Cadmium Orange and Alizarin Crimson. A thin application of Alizarin Crimson and Cadmium Red is washed over the buildings, and French Ultramarine is then added to suggest shadows. The effect is still soft but already a sense of depth is beginning to emerge.

3 Definition is increased further to separate out the objects on the different spatial planes. Light patches are left in the wash on the buildings in the background to suggest structure without going into detail. The distant poles are darkened, while the striped poles are brought forward by applying a dark wash around them. The background is almost complete. The addition of darks has given substance to the bulk of the buildings, which has made the domes and turrets recede.

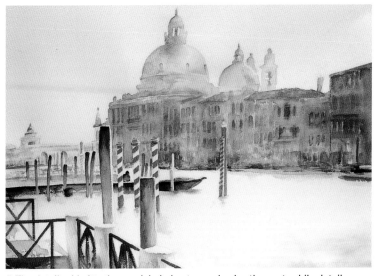

DRAWING THE EYE

4 Strengthening the colours in parts of the foreground focuses the eye there – touches of pure bright Cadmium Red on the parking poles, Burnt Sienna on the near posts and Viridian Green on the boat.

5 The detail added to the gondola helps to emphasize the post, while detail stroked onto the foreground fence gives it solidity and brings it forward in space. Additional darks on the far buildings emphasize the water's edge. The foreground posts have also been darkened, adding to the three-dimensional aspect of the painting. The final picture has a great sense of height and distance, achieved by leaving large expanses of sky and water unpainted, and cleverly using cool and warm colours.

MAKING COLOUR STUDIES

ARTISTS ARE ALWAYS ADVISED TO CARRY A SMALL SKETCHBOOK IN WHICH TO DRAW SUBJECTS THAT CATCH THEIR EYE, AND THAT THEY CAN LATER WORK UP INTO MORE FINISHED PIECES. MAKING COLOUR STUDIES IN YOUR SKETCHBOOK TAKES THE PROCESS ONE STEP FURTHER.

Colour studies fall midway between sketching and painting. When you have the time and concentration to develop a sketch image more fully, colour is often the element that you will want to focus upon in greater detail. For this kind of work, paint is the essential medium, rather than coloured pencils, crayons or pens. The potential for mixing and overlaying colours gives you the necessary degree of subtlety and range of interpretation.

Watercolour is the traditional and most suitable medium for doing colour studies. It is a better choice than gouache because the colours are translucent and do not readily devalue when they blend and mix, and they can be mixed and overlaid directly on the paper surface, building up strength and tone layer upon layer, whereas opaque gouache generally has to be mixed in a palette to achieve accurate colour effects.

However, you may sometimes need what is known as body colour – a degree of opacity – to create particular nuances such as strong highlights or textural detail. Many watercolour boxes include a small tube of opaque white for highlighting, which should always be done at the final stage of a watercolour study.

STUDY TIPS

• An alternative to doing studies in watercolour is to use watercolour pencils. These are easy to carry and the only extra items you will need are some water and a brush to sweep the water across the pencilled marks to transform them into washes.

• Don't be afraid to make written notes on your colour studies. This can provide you with important information that you may need later on.

NOTING THE ESSENTIALS

This deceptively simple colour sketch contains a lot of information that will be of use to the artist later. As well as noting colour and tonal values, the study preserves a strong sense of space and a clear delineation of the relative spatial planes, from the foreground to the distant background.

SPEED VERSUS CONTENT

A quick colour study is a spontaneous response to a subject, and you would not want to lose that spontaneity. However, if a study is to provide useful reference, consideration should go into it. Remember that, because watercolours are translucent, you cannot retrieve a light tone from a dark once you have laid the colour, or overpaint with a paler hue. Spend a little time studying the subject before you start work to establish a general sequence of colours, but do not abandon spontaneity – 'dash in' particular colour effects as you see them.

If you are unsure where to start, identify one hue and work right across your sketchbook page, putting down that hue wherever it occurs in your subject. Work through the next most obvious colour, and so on, until you have woven the general pattern of colours. Then start to develop the image by adjusting the balance of individual hues in relation to one another and overlaying smaller colour areas to achieve more subtlety and depth.

The colour studies on these pages combine that lovely, loose brushwork that so typifies the watercolour medium with useful information on colour and form.

RECORDING LIGHT AND SHADE

Using just a few colours and some simple brushstrokes, the artist has recorded the key elements of this scene. The white highlights on the tree trunk and the shadows snaking across the ground instantly give a sense of the bright sunshine and deep shade that define the subject.

MAKING COLOUR NOTES

Simple outlines and subtle variations of colour in the mass of foliage are recorded here. Colour studies can be useful in simplifying visual information, helping the artist to maintain focus later when working up a study into a painting.

RECORDING AN INITIAL RESPONSE

Despite the speed with which this richly coloured study was made, it still 'reads' as a sunset with foliage and long grass in the foreground. As a record of the artist's initial response to the subject, it is an invaluable aide-memoire, helping her remember what struck her most about the scene and thus what to emphasize in any painting she develops from it.

FINDING YOUR STYLE

THE WAY THAT YOU PAINT AND DRAW, THE MARKS YOU MAKE, THE COLOURS YOU USE AND THE SUBJECTS YOU CHOOSE, MAKE UP YOUR PERSONAL ARTISTIC 'LANGUAGE'. LIKE A CHILD LEARNING TO SPEAK, YOU NEED TIME AND PRACTICE TO DEVELOP YOUR VOCABULARY.

Often, through lack of confidence, beginners will paint the way that they think they should rather than follow their own creative instincts. Even the greatest artists have to begin somewhere and it takes years of practice for them to develop their own personal style. As they become more sure, their work can move from the figurative to the more abstracted. Think of Picasso, for example; his early drawings, produced at a precociously early age, were highly academic and gave little hint at the highly personalized and distinctive style of work that was to come later.

There are several ways to develop your own artistic 'language'. The first, obviously, is practice: draw and paint often, to hone your skills and sharpen your eye. If you feel that you never have enough time to paint, take comfort from the thought that little and often can be a more effective strategy than spending whole days on a painting, with long gaps of time in between. A successful painting requires that you develop a relationship with it, and ideally this requires daily contact – if only just to look at it and assess what to do next (not all creative work occurs on the paper; a lot of it is processed in the mind's eye).

Have a watercolour pad to use for colour sketches, and as a place to explore and experiment. See the pages as a place to play with the medium, to make marks freely without worrying about making 'mistakes'. Really, there are no mistakes, just opportunities for learning. Working quickly and freely can help you to loosen up too, and prevent your style becoming too 'tight'.

Nourish your artist's imagination. Study the work of other artists for ideas and inspiration that might trigger ideas of your own. These examples of the same artist's work, that range from experiments with mark-making and colour sketches to more finished pieces, show just how enjoyable it can be to explore the possibilities offered by watercolour.

EXPLORING A SINGLE SUBJECT
In this lively series of paintings by Brian Innes, the artist has explored the same subject several times, using different colours and different backgrounds to create different effects. Painting the same subject more than once can be a useful way to build a relationship with it, and develop your own painting language in response to it.

EXPERIMENTING WITH WATERCOLOUR

Watercolour offers more techniques to the artist than perhaps any other painting medium. Your watercolour pad, or some spare paper, is the ideal place to explore the kinds of effects you can achieve. In this colour sketch (left) the artist explores his responses to the subject with a range of different marks, techniques and media.

STOP AND REFLECT

To help you assess your painting to see whether it is working and what adjustments to make, hold it up to a mirror and look at it in reverse. This useful trick stops you seeing what you 'know' and gives you a more objective view – even if it is a back-to-front one.

GAINING CONFIDENCE

Colour sketches like this one (above) are the backbone of the artist's repertoire. Not only do they record valuable information, but they also help the artist to 'loosen up' and gain in confidence. In the study of a vase of flowers by a window (right), the artist has not been constrained by idea of what a watercolour 'should' be but has freely mixed the medium with wax resist and black line.

WORKING FROM PHOTOGRAPHS

PHOTOGRAPHS ARE A WONDERFUL REFERENCE FOR PAINTING, AND THERE ARE FEW ARTISTS NOWADAYS WHO DON'T USE A CAMERA. HOWEVER, IT IS IMPORTANT TO REMEMBER THAT THE CAMERA DOESN'T ALWAYS SEE AS WE DO.

When sketching directly from the subject, you may decide to leave out some features and possibly change things around a bit to improve the composition. You should try to do the same with photographs. It is more difficult in this case, however, since a photograph presents only one viewpoint; if you are out in the landscape, you can move around to explore more possibilities. Always bear in mind that painting is about interpretation, not slavish copying. You don't have to follow the same format as the photo; instead, try framing it in different ways using L-shaped pieces of cardboard or paper. You might find that taking the middle section of a landscape-format photograph provides a more unusual vertical composition.

Remember also that there are ways to add to a photograph, such as by putting in more sky or foreground than is actually shown. Wide landscapes or seascapes often benefit from a low horizon, with the sky occupying more than half the picture space, while a large area of foreground has the effect of pushing a focal point back in space to create a stronger feeling of depth and of the image receding. Test this by sticking your photo down on paper and sketching in more sky or foreground with a quick-to-use medium such as pastel.

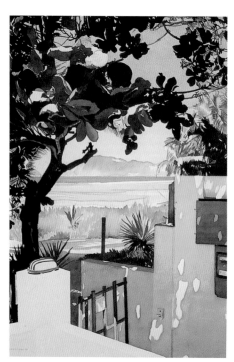

LIGHTENING THE COLOURS
Club del Mar by Linda Kooluris Dobbs
This painting is obviously not a true record of the scene; instead, the artist has drawn on experience and her immediate impressions to heighten the colours while retaining the composition. Notice especially the group of leaves above the broken branch, which are black in the photograph.

EXPLORING POSSIBILITIES
The photograph at the top is rather cluttered, with the expanse of foreground reducing the importance of the building. 'Zooming into' a smaller area in the version above offers a stronger, more effective composition with strong possibilities.

CHANGING THE EMPHASIS

The artist took this photograph (above) mainly to capture the effect of the light on the waves. However, when she looked at it again, she decided that it was unbalanced, so in her painting (right) she extended the sky from her memory in order to achieve a more expansive image.

FOCUSING ON THE SUBJECT

Yellow Daisies by Katrina Small
In the finished painting (below), the artist has been faithful to the colours, shapes and shadows of the flowers in the photograph (bottom). However, she has chosen to give the painted version a much more blurry, and colourful, background, which throws the daisies into greater relief.

EDITING THE IMAGE

Blue Skies by Sue Kemp
Here, the artist was interested as much in the light effects as in the rocks, and she has departed radically from the more uniform colours of the photograph. She has also given more emphasis to the rocks by increasing their height, and has improved the composition by including clouds that balance this dominant feature and also give a sense of movement.

COMPOSITION

COMPOSITION IS THE ARRANGEMENT
OF ELEMENTS WITHIN A SPACE,
AND GOOD COMPOSITION IS
ESSENTIAL TO ANY PAINTING.

Creating a successful painting is about more than the subject matter you choose and the colours and techniques you use – it needs to be well composed too. A pleasing composition will appear harmonious and balanced, with all the elements working together to create an eye-catching scene.

To put it simply, 'composition' refers to the way in which all the parts of your painting work together: where the subject matter is placed within the space, how the space is divided up and how these two aspects work in relation to the format you have chosen (landscape or portrait, square or rectangular). A well-composed picture is likely to look more accomplished and professional and there are certain principles, explained on these two pages, that will help you achieve that.

It can also be helpful to examine the composition of paintings you like, and try to analyse why they work. You can then apply the same approach to your own work.

LEADING THE EYE
A good composition should contain visual passages that lead the viewer's eye into and around the entire painting. A great way to create a visual passage in a painting is to incorporate diagonal and curved lines that lead the eye to the centre of interest. In this photograph, the diagonal rows of lavender lead the eye directly to the distant sunlit village.

DETERMINING THE FOCUS
Every composition needs a focal point, or centre of interest. A focal point can be something obvious like a person or an object, or it can be more subtle, like gleaming highlights on the side of a hill or a pattern of shadows on a street. In this photograph, the colourful reflections are so compelling that they become the focus of the painting.

THE RULE OF THIRDS
Once you've established a focal point, it's important to place it correctly within the scene. A good way to do this is to follow the rule of thirds. Divide the painting surface into thirds horizontally and vertically; then place your focal point (in this case, the tree) at or near one of the points where the lines intersect. This keeps your centre of interest away from the extremes – corners, dead centre or at the very top or bottom of the composition.

CREATING CONTRAST
The eye is drawn towards areas of strong contrasts in tonal value as well as to pure colour, so your composition should include a variety of light, medium and dark values to help direct the viewer's eye. In this photo, the brightly lit side of the right-hand pear contrasts with the dark background, attracting immediate attention.

Cropping a picture

Sometimes a picture works better if you 'crop' or frame the image differently – rather like zooming in or out with a camera lens. This example, of a photo of a man reading in a café, shows how cropping the picture differently strengthens the composition.

WIDE VIEW

1 In the original photo the view is quite wide. The eye is drawn to the man at the table because this is the most interesting part of the picture, but there is a lot of space to his left that is distracting and adds nothing to the composition.

2 The red square imposed on the photo shows how it could be cropped more effectively.

3 Eliminating the left side and most of the background of the original photograph makes the scene tighter, closer and more intimate, and focuses in on the part of the image that the eye is drawn to anyway.

MAKE A VIEWFINDER

A viewfinder is a useful tool for identifying a good composition and is easy to make. Cut two L-shapes from cardboard and paperclip them together to form a square or a rectangle. Look at your scene through the viewfinder – bring it closer and hold it out further, move it around the scene and make the opening wider and narrower until you find a pleasing composition.

ENLARGING YOUR DRAWING

IT IS NOT ALWAYS NECESSARY TO BEGIN A PAINTING WITH A DETAILED DRAWING, BUT SOME SUBJECTS, SUCH AS PORTRAITS, CALL FOR A CAREFUL, METHODICAL APPROACH IN THE EARLY STAGES.

One way of avoiding too much drawing and erasing on the paper, which can spoil the surface, is to make a smaller study of the subject first and then transfer it to the watercolour paper by squaring it up to the size desired. A photograph can be used instead of a drawing, but photographs do tend to flatten and distort perspective, and sometimes present an insufficiently clear image, so try to use them only in conjunction with sketches, observation and imagination.

Squaring up is a slightly laborious process, but it isn't too difficult and really does pay off when the effect of the painting depends on accuracy.

Using a ruler, draw a measured grid over the study or photograph, then draw another grid on the watercolour paper, using light pencil marks. This must have the same number of squares, but if you want to enlarge the drawing, they must obviously be larger. If you use a 2.5cm (1in) grid for your original drawing and a 3.8cm (1½in) one for the painting, it will be one-and-a-half times the size, and so on. When the grid is complete, look carefully at the drawing, note where each line intersects a grid line and transfer the information from one to the other.

USING A SQUARED-UP GRID

1 The method shown here avoids damaging the original drawing or photograph. A grid is drawn with a fibre-tipped pen on a sheet of acetate. The grid is traced from a sheet of graph paper beneath it, which saves time and is very accurate.

2 The next stage is drawing an enlarged version of the grid on the working paper. Pencil, T-square and ruler are needed for this, and the pencil lines of the transferred grid should be as faint as possible.

3 The acetate sheet is then placed over the photograph or working drawing (far left), and the image is transferred to the working paper square by square (left). This process should not be rushed and the work should be checked carefully as it progresses, or part of the composition could be placed in the wrong square.

DIVIDING A SQUARED-UP GRID INTO SMALLER UNITS

Dividing the squares up diagonally into triangles breaks the original image up into even smaller segments, thus providing an even more exact grid to work from.

TIPS: OTHER METHODS OF TRANSFERRING

There are other methods you can use to transfer your preliminary drawing.

• You can photocopy it, enlarging or reducing it to the size you want. Trace the copy, then trace this onto the sheet or other support on which you will be painting. This will work for paintings up to A3 size.

• Use a pantograph – a handy instrument available from art shops. The arm of the pantograph consists of criss-crossing strips of wood or other material that can concertina up or down, rather like a garden trellis, allowing you to reduce or enlarge your drawing in exact proportion to the original.

USING A GRID TO DRAW A LANDSCAPE

In this example, an acetate grid is laid over a photograph of a woodland scene. A grid is lightly drawn in pencil on a piece of paper. The information in each square of the acetate grid is copied across one square at a time. As long as your grid lines are faint, they will be covered by your paint or they can be erased when the painting is complete.

ORDER OF WORKING

BECAUSE THERE ARE NO RIGID RULES IN WATERCOLOUR PAINTING, IT CAN BE HARD TO KNOW HOW TO BEGIN. THE DIAGRAMS INDICATE A POSSIBLE ORDER OF WORKING, STARTING WITH THE LIGHTEST AREAS AND FINISHING WITH THE DARKEST.

It isn't always easy to decide where and how to begin a painting. The standard advice about watercolour is that because the colours are transparent, you have to work 'from light to dark'. This means that when putting colour on in layers, you must begin with the lightest ones, because you can only make colours darker by adding a layer. But it does not mean that you must always start with the palest bit of picture.

Suppose you're painting a bunch of white flowers in a dark blue vase against a light blue background. The conventional method would be to lay a light blue wash over the vase and background, reserving the flowers and any highlights as white paper, let this dry and then paint the vase on top. But you could begin with the vase, and paint the background around it. Some artists prefer to put down areas of dark colour first, because this gives them a point of reference for the rest of the picture.

Whichever method you choose, your first task is to anaylse your subject in terms of light and dark blocks of colour. Look at the photographs on these pages and see whether you can figure out which colours you would put on first. Then compare this with the sequences in the numbered diagrams which give a suggested order of work.

PAINTING BUILDINGS

1 First make a drawing, then lay a flat or graded blue wash for the sky and leave it to dry. Lay a very pale wash, perhaps Yellow Ochre with a touch of Alizarin Crimson, over the rest of the painting.

2 Paint the shadowed side of the building, then begin to darken the colours in the central area and foreground shadow. Paint the lamp post over the colours.

3 Add further dark washes to the central area and the foreground shadow, and then begin to build up detail on the buildings.

4 Continue to add detail and strengthen colours where necessary.

PAINTING A LANDSCAPE

1 Draw the main shapes. Lay a pale wash for the sky and a slightly darker one for the distant hills. Lay ochre washes over the main areas of the painting, but not the river. If blue is painted over ochre it will turn green.

2 Paint the river with a mid-blue wash.

3 Start on all the green areas, painting over the ochre washes. Begin in the distance with pale washes, building to darker colour in the foreground.

4 With all areas blocked in, gradually add detail and strengthen colours, reserving ochre highlights in the foreground.

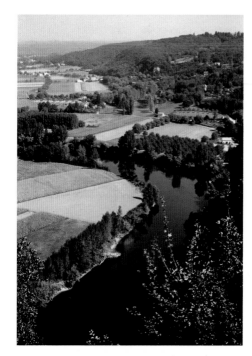

PAINTING A STILL LIFE

1 Make an outline drawing, then lay a light yellow-brown wash over the background, reserving the white flowers, and leave to dry.

2 Lay separate washes for the vase and the blue pot.

3 Block in the checked cloth with blue, reserving white squares. Block in the main shapes of the leaves, painting individual leaves over the background wash.

4 Begin to add detail and continue to darken colour where necessary.

INDEX

ACKNOWLEDGMENTS

Quarto would like to thank **Winsor & Newton** for supplying materials for photography. We would also like to thank the following artists for kindly supplying images for inclusion in this book:

Denny Bond www.dennybondillustration.com

Catherine Brennand
www.catherinebrennand.co.uk

Clare Brooks Member of Islington Arts Club

Allan Brown

Julia Cassels www.juliacassels.com

David Castle www.davidcastleart.com

Moira Clinch www.londonart.co.uk

Marjorie Collins www.marjoriecollins.com

Paul Dawson

Linda Kooluris Dobbs www.koolurisdobbs.ca

Joe Dowden www.joedowden.net

Ray Evans www.manorhousegallery.co.uk

D.R Ganthorpe BWS, FIGA
www.northorpe-watercolour-society.co.uk

Sarah Garvey sarah@sgarvey.co.uk

Elizabeth Haines www.elizabethhaines.co.uk

Tracy Hall www.watercolour-artist.co.uk

Jan Hart for her contribution to the color articles

Lisa Hill www.lisahillwatercolorist.com

Shari Hills www.sharihills.co.uk

Moira Huntly www.manorhousegallery.co.uk

Brian Innes

Terry Jarvis www.terryjarvis.com

Ronald Jesty

Sue Kemp www.suekemp.com

Keith M. Kennedy

Charles Knight RWS, ROI

Jeanne Lamar www.jeannelamar.com

Heather Maunders
www.heathermaunders.com

Adrienne Pavelka www.adrienne-pavelka.com

Roger Pickett www.rogerpickett-artist.com

David Poxon www.davidpoxon.co.uk

Sally Robertson www.sallyrobertson.com

Mary Ann Rogers www.marogers.com

Katrina Small www.katrinasmallstudios.com

Ann Smith www.annsmithwatercolors.com

Jake Sutton www.jakesutton.co.uk

Carolyn Wilson www.carolynwilsonartist.com